Windows & Doors

Ron Hazelton, chief consultant for **HOW TO FIX IT**, is the Home Improvement Editor for ABC-TV's *Good Morning America* and host of his own home improvement series, Ron Hazelton's *HouseCalls*. He has produced and hosted more than 200 episodes of *The House Doctor*, a home-improvement series airing on the *Home and Garden Television Network* (HGTV).

On television, and in real life, Ron is a coach who visits people in their own homes, helping them do things for themselves. He pioneered the concept of on-location, home-improvement television, making over 600 televised house calls, doing real-life projects with real people.

The son of a building contractor, Ron has always had a fascination with the home and how it works. He left a successful career as a marketing executive to learn woodworking, eventually becoming a Master Craftsman and cabinetmaker. In 1978, he founded Cow Hollow Woodworks in San Francisco, an antique restoration workshop that restored over 17,000 pieces of furniture during his tenure.

Dave Gibiser, Glazier and Window Repair Specialist has spent the last decade repairing every imaginable type of window and door for *Pioneer Glass & Mirror* located in Eastern Pennsylvania. Dave specializes in thermopane windows and splits his time evenly between the shop and on-site installations.

Ed Maila, a Master Carpenter on Long Island, owns his own construction company, *Millcoast Woodwrights*. His work varies from highly specialized projects like dock building and furniture construction to everyday home renovations. Some of his more challenging improvements include custom-built windows and doors.

Windows & Doors

By The Editors of Time-Life Books, Alexandria, Virginia

With **TRADE SECRETS** From **Ron Hazelton**

Contents

FIX IT: Double-Hung Windows

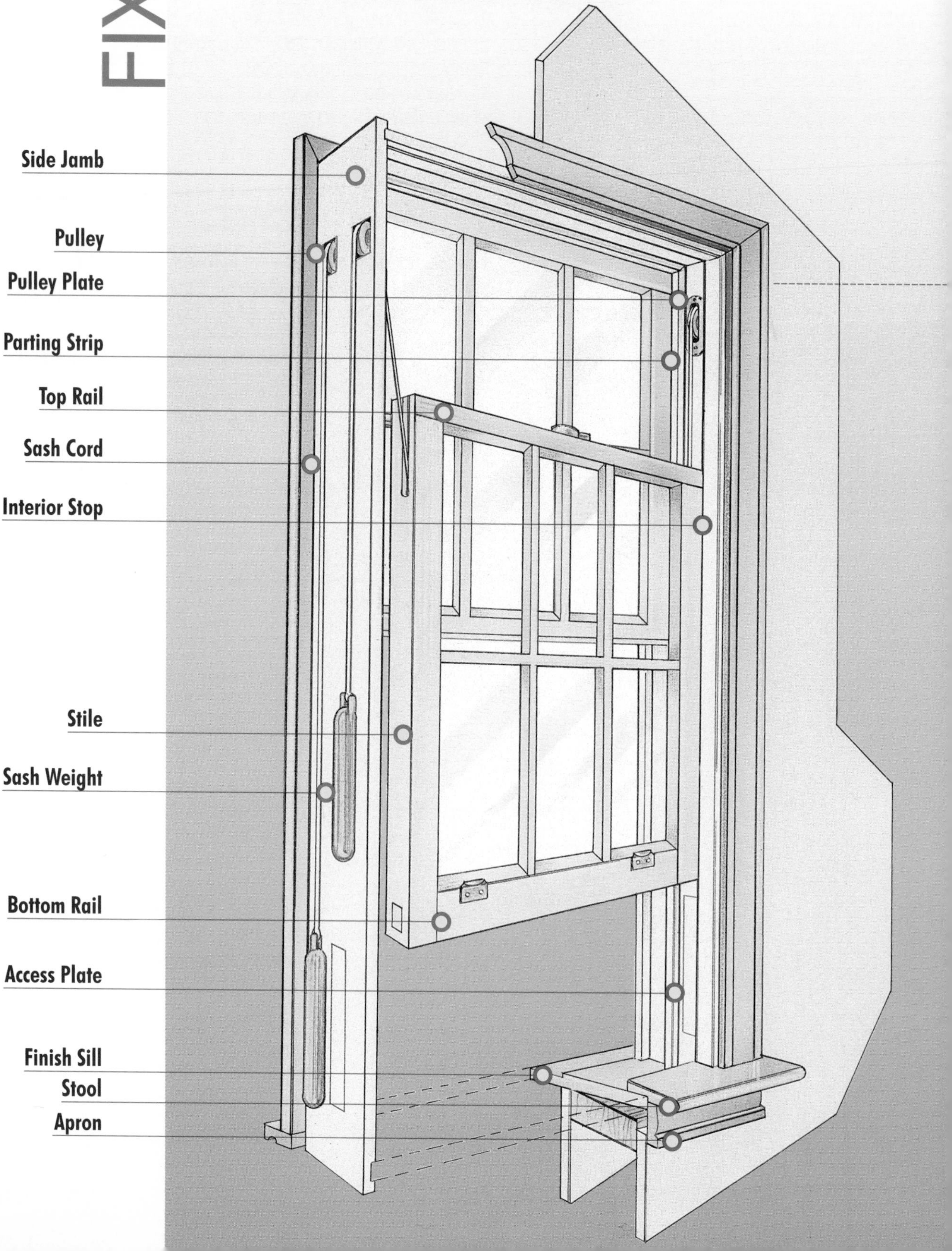

Side Jamb

Pulley

Pulley Plate

Parting Strip

Top Rail

Sash Cord

Interior Stop

Stile

Sash Weight

Bottom Rail

Access Plate

Finish Sill

Stool

Apron

Contents

How They Work

A typical double-hung window consists of a movable upper and lower sash, channels for the sashes to slide in, and a balance system that allows either sash to open and close with a light touch. (Single-hung windows, on which only the lower sash is movable, work similarly and are maintained the same way.)

In older houses, you'll most often encounter double-hung windows constructed of wood and balanced by a weight-and-pulley system that's hidden in a pocket in the wall *(left)*. To get at the weights and sash cord for repair, look for an access plate positioned near the bottom of each sash channel.

Newer windows are rarely equipped with a weight-and-pulley system. Instead, they have a block-and-tackle system, one operated by a clockspring, or a third called a spiral balance system. All three systems are described on page 12.

Troubleshooting

Problem	Solution
• **Window doesn't open or opens with difficulty**	Break paint bond between sash and stop, or meeting rails **10** • Strip paint buildup in channels **11** • Reposition interior stop if warped **12** • Plane warped sash **13** • Replace broken sash chain **18** • Replace old balance with a clockspring balance **19** • Install replacement channels **21** • Replace old balance with a spiral balance **22** • Replace faulty block-and-tackle balance **24** • Adjust or replace faulty spiral balance **22** • Replace faulty clockspring balance **19** •
• **Lower sash doesn't stay open**	Replace broken sash chain **18** • Replace old balance with clockspring balance **19** • Install replacement channels **21** • Replace old balance with a spiral balance **22** • Replace faulty block-and-tackle balance **24** • Adjust or replace faulty spiral balance **22** • Replace faulty clockspring balance **19** •
• **Wood sash rattles**	Replace wood interior stop if shrunk or deteriorated **12** • Reinforce loose sash joints **14** • Replace sill or sash if rotted **15** • Install weather stripping **118** •

Before You Start

Most of the problems with double-hung windows don't become evident until someone tries to open or close the sash.

There may well be a simple solution to the problem. Since windows are continuously exposed to the elements, it's easy for dirt and debris to get packed into the gaps between the sash and the channels. A thorough cleaning with mild soap and a brush will often restore a window to smooth operation. For continuing smooth operation, lubricate the channels with paraffin to help keep them clean and dry.

Before undertaking any other repair, identify the balance system. Sash cords and pulleys indicate a weight-and-pulley system; a small tube running the length of the sash channel identifies a spiral balance; and a steel tape running in the sash channel lets you know you're dealing with a clockspring balance. If the window is aluminum, it almost certainly features a block-and-tackle balance.

Finally, keep in mind that if you need to remove the upper sash in an older balance system, it's usually necessary to first remove the lower sash.

Before You Start Tips:

···⳽ Don't begin any window repair job before checking the weather forecast, particularly if you need to remove the sash. Be prepared with plastic sheeting to cover the opening if a storm blows in.

···⳽ If you remove a sash, set it safely aside where you won't accidentally kick the glass and shatter it.

TOOLS

Utility knife
Putty knife
Pry bar
Paint scraper
Heat gun
Cold chisel
Pliers
Handsaw
Jack plane
C-clamps
Router
Chisel
Electric drill
Spiral-balance adjusting tool

MATERIALS

Dowels
Shims
Finishing nails
Replacement sash cord
New balance system
Replacement sash channels

SAFETY FIRST

Wear eye protection when nailing. For demolition work, such as removing trim, sash channels, or sills, protect yourself with both gloves and saftey glasses.

Unbinding a Wood Sash

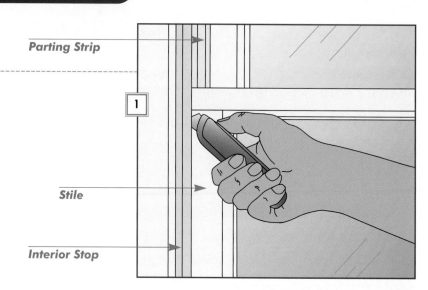

Parting Strip

Stile

Interior Stop

1. BREAKING A PAINT BOND

- Slice through the paint bond with a utility knife *(right)*, taking care not to gouge either the stop or the sash.

- Cut the paint wherever the sash makes contact with a stop, a parting strip, the window sill, or the other sash.

- If the window still won't open, continue to Steps 2 and 3. If it opens with difficulty, go to Step 4 or 5.

2. SEPARATING STOP FROM SASH

- Wedge a pair of putty knives between the stop and stile, and drive them apart with a cold chisel and a hammer *(right)*. Repeat the procedure up and down the window.

- If the window doesn't open, separate the sash from the parting strips.

- For windows that still will not open, go to Step 3.

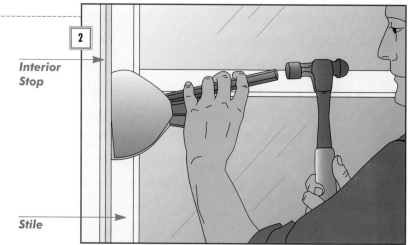

Interior Stop

Stile

Ron's TRADE SECRETS

CUSTOMIZING A COLD CHISEL
I had mixed results whenever I used a pair of putty knives and a cold chisel to open a stubborn window. The problem? There was little space between the putty knives for the chisel. To ease this overcrowding, I reground the business end of my cold chisel into a long, smooth taper *(near right)*. I also discovered that rubbing a little paraffin onto the chisel helps it slip easily between the putty knives and force them apart.

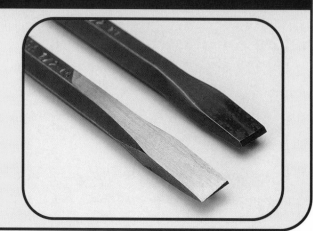

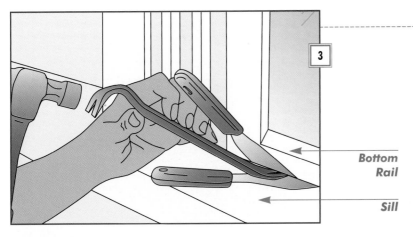

Bottom
Rail

Sill

3. FORCING UP THE SASH

• Outside, wedge two putty knives between the sill and the sash's bottom rail near a corner. Drive the knives apart with a utility bar and a hammer *(left)*. Alternate working on each corner to free the sash.

• If this fails, remove the sash *(page 12)* and if necessary, strip the channels *(below)* or plane the sash *(page 13)*.

 CAUTION: *Hammer gently; too much force may separate the sash joints.*

4. SCRAPING A SASH CHANNEL

• Work the sash upward as far as it will go.

• If the paint in the channels is thick and bumpy, remove it with a paint scraper *(left)*.

• When scraping doesn't succeed, proceed to Step 5.

5. STRIPPING A SASH CHANNEL

If many layers of paint cover the channel, they may not come off without assistance from a heat gun.

• Point the heat gun at a small area until the paint just begins to blister *(left)*. Then scrape up the softened paint with a narrow putty knife.

• After all the paint is gone, sand and repaint the channels.

• Finish the job by lubricating the channels with paraffin or a silicone spray.

Removing Upper and Lower Sashes

1. PRYING OFF AN INTERIOR STOP

• If the window has a spiral balance *(side-bar, below)*, unscrew its tube from the top of the jamb and its mounting bracket from the bottom rail before prying off the stops.

• Break any paint bond between the stop and jamb *(page 10, Step 1)*.

• Push two putty knives between the stop and the jamb, and drive them apart with a cold chisel and hammer *(right)*. Start at the middle of the stop and work up and down.

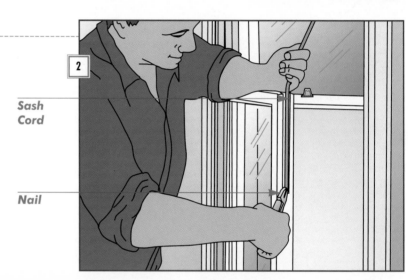

Cold Chisel

Putty Knife

Interior Stop

2. REMOVING THE LOWER SASH

• Pull the sash out of the frame on the side where you removed the stop.

• Remove any screws or nails securing the sash cord to the sash *(right)*. Push a nail through the cord to prevent it from slipping past the pulley.

• Lift out the other side of the window and remove the cord in the same way.

• If the balance is a clockspring, unhook the tape from the sash and feed it back to the drum.

Sash Cord

Nail

THREE TYPES OF BALANCES

Block-and-Tackle Balance

Typical of aluminum-window balances, this model rides in a groove in the stile and attaches to the jamb with a clip on top and a hook on the bottom. You cannot adjust its tension. Hangs in a tube connected to the top of the jamb.

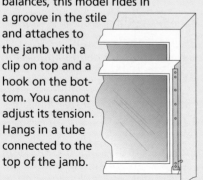

Spiral Balance

The spiral connects either to a bracket on the sash *(below)* or into a plastic block that rides in the sash channel. You can adjust the tension of both types.

Clockspring Balance

Usually mounted on the side jamb, it operates by means of a small steel tape fastened to a bracket on the sash. It is weight-specific but can be adjusted plus or minus 2 pounds.

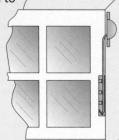

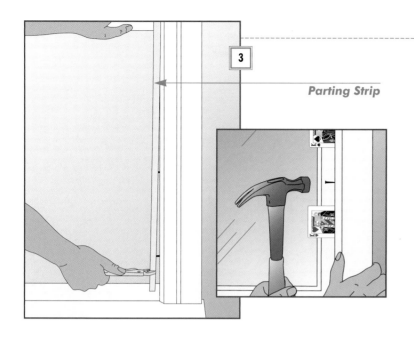

Parting Strip

3. REMOVING THE UPPER SASH

• If the window has a spiral balance, support the sash with a board, then disengage the balance *(Step 1)*.

• Remove the parting strip from the side where you removed the interior stop.

• Pull the bottom of the strip out of its groove in the jamb with locking-grip pliers padded by wood shims *(left)*.

• Lower the upper sash and remove it as you did the lower sash in Step 2.

• After completing the repair, reassemble by reversing the disassembly steps. To allow the sash to move freely when re-installing the stops, use playing cards as spacers *(inset)*.

Correcting a Warped Sash

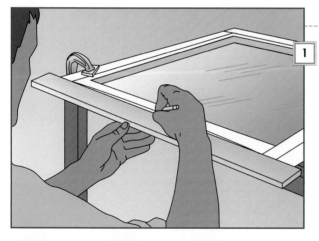

1. MARKING THE WARP

• Remove the binding sash from its frame *(page 12)* and clamp it to a work table.

• Align a straightedge along the warped side of the stile and draw a line indicating the warp *(left)*.

• Flatten a slight warp with sandpaper wrapped around a block of wood. For a more pronounced warp, shave away the binding area with a plane *(Step 2)*.

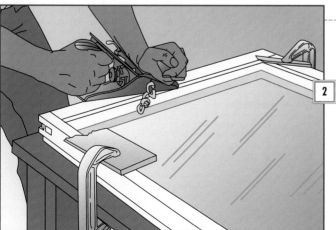

2. PLANING THE SASH

• Set a jack plane for a fine cut. Holding the plane firmly in both hands, push it over the warped area, going with the grain *(left)*.

• To prevent gouging the sash, lift the front of the plane off the wood as you finish the stroke. After each stroke, check the line that marks the warp.

• Sand the sash smooth once you've flattened it with the plane, then touch up the paint or varnish.

Reinforcing the Joints of a Wood Sash

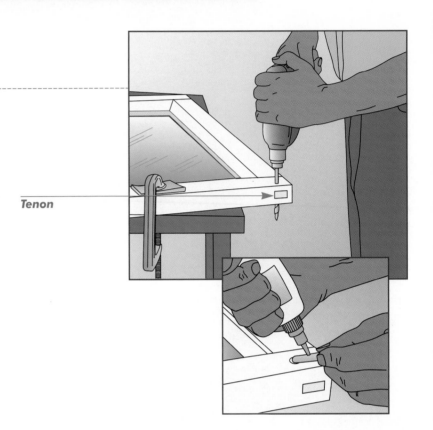

DOWELING A SASH JOINT

● Remove the sash *(page 12)* and clamp it to a work table so the weak joint extends over the edge.

● With a drill and a 1/4-inch bit, bore a hole through the tenon *(right)*.

● Cut a 1/4-inch dowel slightly longer than the thickness of the sash.

● Apply glue to the dowel *(inset)* and drive it into the hole with a hammer.

● When the glue is dry, sand the dowel flush.

Tenon

WEDGE FOR EXTRA STRENGTH

● Remove the sash *(page 12)* and clamp it to a work table.

● From the thin end of a cedar shim, cut a wedge the width of the tenon and 1-1/2 inches long.

● Coat both sides of the wedge with carpenter's glue and tap it into the joint next to the tenon with a hammer *(right)*.

● When the glue is dry, sand the wedge flush.

 CAUTION: *Go gently when tapping in the wedge; too much force can crack the sash.*

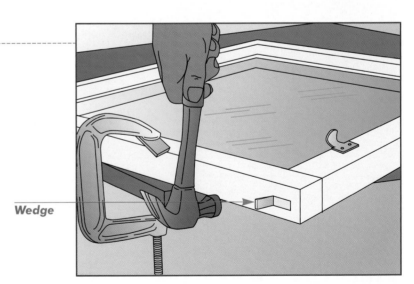

Wedge

A New Window Sill

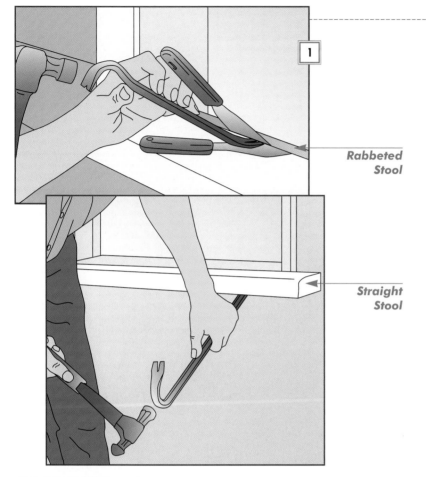

1

Rabbeted Stool

Straight Stool

2

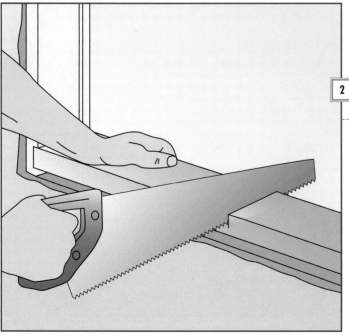

1. REMOVING A STOOL

There are two types of stools: rabbeted and straight. A rabbeted stool *(page 6)* overlaps the indoor edge of the sill. A straight stool is nailed flush to the sill.

● In order to gain access to either type of sill, first remove the window's interior stops *(page 10)*. Then pry off the side trim and apron as for a door *(page 52)*. If the trim corners are nailed together, pry each one as a unit.

● To remove a rabbeted stool *(left, top)*, go outside and wedge a pair of wide putty knives between the sill and the stool, and drive them apart with a utility bar and a hammer.

● For a straight stool *(left, bottom)*, free it from the sill with a hammer and a pry bar.

● Go outside and dislodge the stool. If the window is inaccessible from the ground, work from inside the house, leaning out the window.

2. CUTTING THE SILL

● If the sill is rotted, measure the width and thickness of the sill and its length both inside and outside. The difference in length is the combined length of the sill horns you'll need for Step 5. The difference in the two widths indicates the width of the horns.

● Using a crosscut saw, cut through the finish sill in two places *(left)*.

3. PRYING OUT THE FINISH SILL

- With a pry bar, lever the middle portion of the sill up and out.

- Gently lift up the two remaining sections *(right).* Pull these pieces free by hand to avoid damaging the jambs, and keep them as a template for a new sill *(Step 4).*

- After you have removed the sill, cut off any protruding nails with a mini-hacksaw *(inset).*

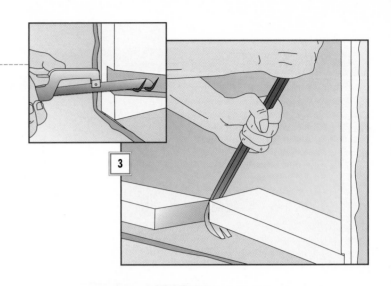

3

4. CUTTING HORNS FOR THE NEW SILL

- Buy sill stock to match the old sill.

- For a rotted sill, use the measurements from Step 2 to lay out the horns. Otherwise, arrange the pieces from Step 3 on the new stock, placing the saw between them as a spacer and noting the location of the drip groove. Outline the shape on the stock.

- Cut out the horns for the new sill *(right).*

- Sand any rough edges smooth.

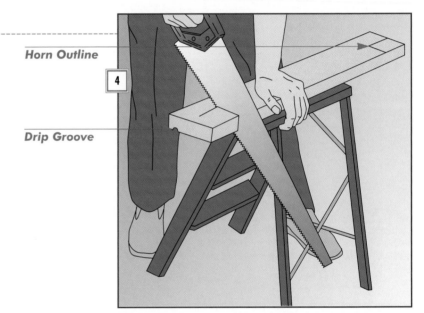

Horn Outline

4

Drip Groove

Ron's **TRADE SECRETS**

DEALING WITH PROTRUDING NAILS

Anytime you take on a window- or door-renovation project, you'll need to remove old nails. A hammer or pry bar works great if the head of the nail is exposed. If the head is broken off or the tip of the nail is exposed, you can use a mini-hacksaw *(top inset)* or even a pair of locking-grip pliers *(right).* Just lock the pliers on the nail and bend the nail back and forth until it snaps off.

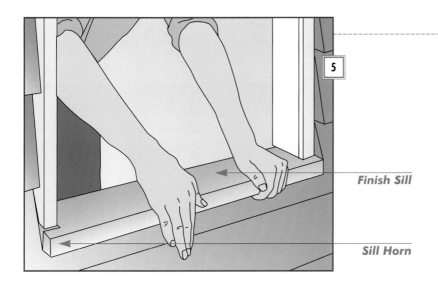

Finish Sill

Sill Horn

5. INSERTING THE SILL

• Vacuum the rough sill at the bottom of the widow opening, as well as any dadoes for the sills in the jambs.

• Hold the sill outside the window and slide it into the dadoes *(left)*. When necessary, tap the sill into place with a rubber mallet and a block of wood.

• If the ends of the sill are too thick for the dadoes, sand the ends with medium-grit sandpaper around a sanding block.

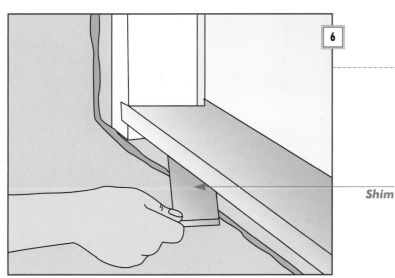

Shim

6. SHIMMING THE SILL

• To support the sill, insert wood shims snugly beneath the center of the sill *(left)*.

• If the sill butts against the jamb or fits in rabbets rather than dadoes, shim the full length of the sill.

⚠️ **CAUTION:** *Take care not to force the sill out of alignment when inserting shims.*

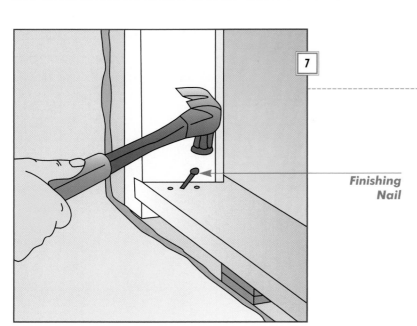

Finishing Nail

7. TOENAILING THE SILL

• Drill pilot holes and then toenail each end of the sill to its jamb with three or four finishing nails *(left)*.

• Caulk all exterior joints between the sill and the window frame *(page 115)*, then re-install the stool, stops, interior trim, and apron.

• Finally, apply exterior paint or varnish to the sill.

Replacing a Broken Sash Chain

1. REMOVING THE ACCESS PLATE

• To find the length of a replacement chain—these instructions also apply to replacing a sash cord—measure from the top of the pulley to the stool and add 6 inches.

• Unscrew the access plate in the sash channel on the side of the broken chain *(right)*. When screws aren't visible, the plate may be nailed shut; pry the nail out with a screwdriver. If there is no plate, remove the window trim to expose the weights and cord.

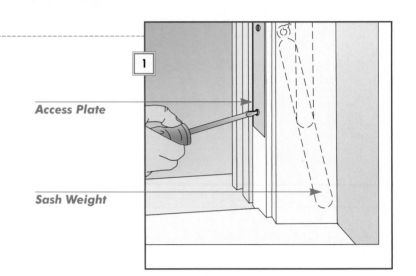

Access Plate

Sash Weight

2. FEEDING THE CHAIN

• Remove the weight and detach the chain.

• Tie a nail or screw to a piece of string to serve as a weight. Feed the weighted end of the string over the pulley and down into the pocket.

• Tie the unweighted end of the string to one end of the new chain, and push a nail through the other end to prevent the chain from slipping past the pulley.

• Pull the string through the access opening until the chain appears *(right)*.

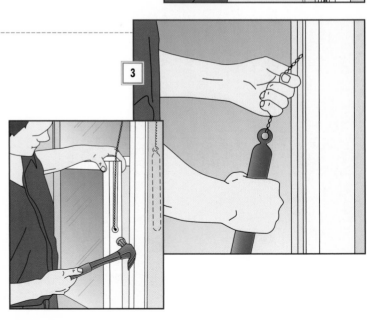

Replacement Chain

String

3. CONNECTING THE CHAIN OR CORD

• Untie the string from the chain, secure it to the weight, and put the weight back in place *(right)*.

• Pull the free end of the chain until the weight hits the pulley. Run a nail though the chain and rest it across the pulley hole.

• Rest the sash on the sill, feed the free end of the chain into the sash groove, and secure it with nails *(inset)* or screws.

• Remove the nail in the chain; raise and hold the sash in place. Adjust the chain's length as needed for the weight to hang 3 inches above the sill. Re-install the access plate.

Replacing a Clockspring Balance

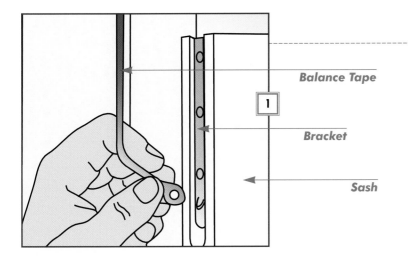

Balance Tape

1

Bracket

Sash

1. UNHOOKING THE BALANCE TAPE

• Take out the sash *(page 12)* and unhook the balance tape from its bracket on the sash *(left)*.

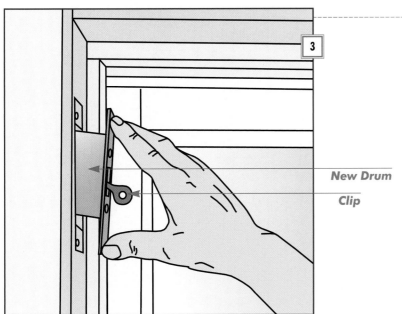

Clockspring Plate

Adjusting Screw

2

2. REMOVING A CLOCKSPRING BALANCE

• Remove the screws securing the clockspring plate to the jamb *(left)* and pull the clockspring drum free of its pocket.

• Take the drum to a window specialist and buy an exact replacement.

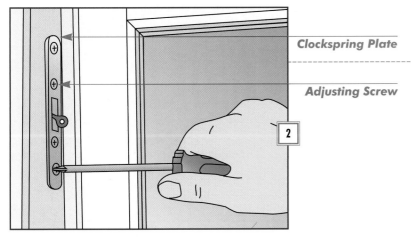

3

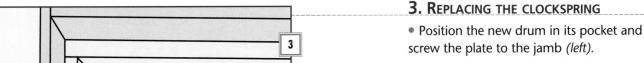

New Drum

Clip

3. REPLACING THE CLOCKSPRING

• Position the new drum in its pocket and screw the plate to the jamb *(left)*.

• Place the sash on the sill, angled out slightly on the side of the new balance.

• With one hand holding the sash, pull down the balance tape clip with the other hand and attach it to the bracket on the side of the sash.

• Reinstall the sash.

• Although the new balance is weight-specific, it can be adjusted plus or minus 2 pounds. To increase the balance tension, turn the adjusting screws *(Step 2)* clockwise, counterclockwise to decrease tension.

Replacement Sash Channels

1. TRIMMING THE PARTING STRIPS

• Measure vertically from the top of the jamb to the outer edge of the sill to determine the length of channel needed.

• Remove the sashes *(page 12)* and the old balance system. (Replacement channels hold the sashes up with friction.)

• Chisel 1/2 inch off each end of the top parting strip *(right)*.

• To install channels on a typical 1-3/8-inch-thick sash, skip to Step 3. If your sash is thicker than this, go to Step 2.

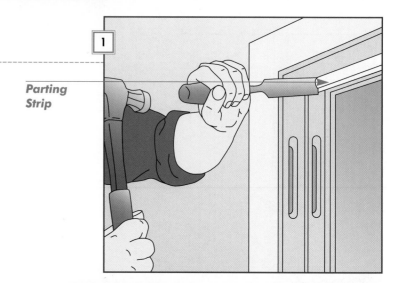

Parting Strip

2. ROUTING THE SASH

Cut rabbets to fit replacement channels in the interior side of the lower sash and exterior side of the upper sash.

• Fit a router with a 1/4-inch rabbet bit, and clamp the sash to a work table.

• Set the edge of the guide so it's flush with the router bearing, then measure the sash thickness and subtract 1-3/8 inches to determine the depth to cut.

• Cut the shaded area to this depth in 1/4-inch increments. For each pass, move the router slowly along the stile *(right)*.

Guide

3. FITTING THE REPLACEMENT CHANNELS

• Hold the upper and lower sashes together, with the exterior side of the lower sash against the interior side of the upper sash.

• Fit the replacement channels along the sash stiles, angled ends down *(right)*. The parting strip—spring-loaded in the model shown here—fits between the sashes, and the channels' flanges act as stops.

Replacement Channel

Parting Strip

4. POSITIONING REPLACEMENT CHANNELS

● Lift the sashes and replacement channels onto the window sill. Tilt them into the window frame, centering them in the old channels *(left)*.

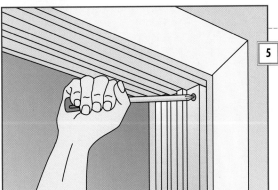

5. ATTACHING CHANNELS WITH SCREWS

● Secure the channels to the jamb with the screws or nails supplied with the kit *(left)*.

● If you routed the sash stiles to fit the replacement channels, re-install the interior stops to hide the grooves.

Ron's TRADE SECRETS

INSULATING SASH POCKETS

Replacement channels are a terrific way to rid yourself of stubborn sashes that constantly bind and stick. But before you install the new channels, it's a good idea to stuff some fiberglass insulation in the pocket to prevent drafts and to help insulate the window as much as possible.

   To reach the pocket, remove the pulley plates from their mortises and the access plates. Then, with a screwdriver or a narrow putty knife, fill the void with insulation *(right)*. Reinstall the access plates before adding the new channels.

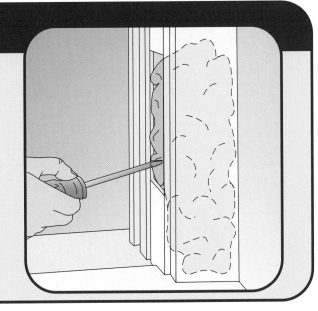

Installing a Spiral Balance

1. PATCHING THE JAMB

• Take out the sashes *(page 12)* and the old balance system. With a chisel and a hammer, square the corners of the mortise left from the old balance system.

• To patch a mortise, first measure the mortise and draw its outline on a 1/4-inch-thick piece of wood. Cut out the patch with a handsaw and glue it into the mortise.

• When the glue is dry, chisel the patch flush with the jamb *(right)*, sand it smooth, and touch it up with paint.

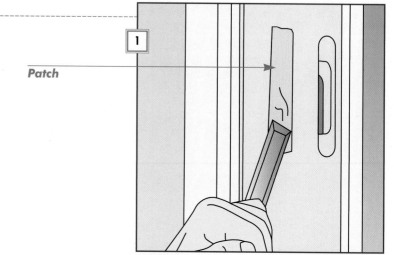

Patch

2. ROUTING GROOVES IN THE SASH

To adapt a wood sash for a spiral balance, rout a groove into each stile.

• Clamp the sash with the stile you are working on facing up, and draw a line down the center of the stile. Set the router guide to center the bit on the line.

• Measure the spiral balance tube's width and select a straight router bit to match.

• Rout the stile in a series of shallow passes until you reach the desired depth *(right)*.

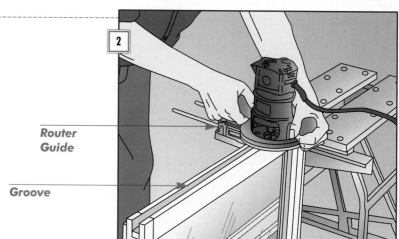

Router Guide

Groove

3. INSTALLING THE MECHANISM

• Re-install the upper sash and parting strip.

• Insert the bottom end of the spiral balance in the stile's groove; the spiral will drop down *(right)*.

• Center the balance in the channel and screw it in place. Repeat for the other side.

• Raise the sash about a foot, rest it on a block of wood, and rotate the mounting bracket near the corner of each sash's bottom until it rises to the rail *(inset)*. Screw each bracket bottom to the sash.

• Repeat this procedure for the lower sash.

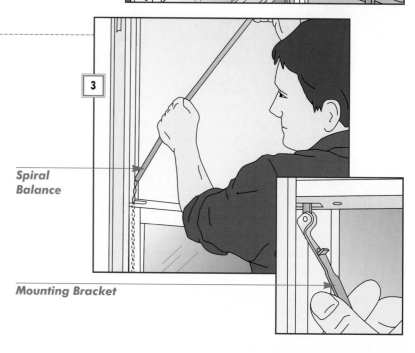

Spiral Balance

Mounting Bracket

Adjusting and Replacing a Spiral Balance

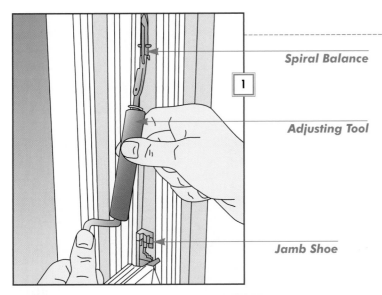

Spiral Balance

1

Adjusting Tool

Jamb Shoe

1. ADJUSTING A SPIRAL BALANCE

When a window with spiral balances misbehaves, try adjusting the balances *(left)*. If the problem persists, one or both balances may need replacing; skip to Step 2.

• Release the slide catches on the sash and tilt the sash indoors.

• Unhook the balance from the jamb shoe with a spiral-balance adjusting tool *(below)*.

• For windows that are hard to open or close, decrease tension by rotating the tool counterclockwise a few turns. If the window won't stay open, turn clockwise.

2

2. REMOVING THE SASHES

To remove a broken balance, you'll first need to remove the sashes.

• Tilt the sash until it is level, then raise one side of the sash to free the corner pivot from the shoe *(left)*. Lift out the other side and store the sash in a safe place. Lower the upper sash and remove it the same way.

• Unhook the broken balance from the jamb shoe with the spiral-balance adjusting tool.

SPIRAL-BALANCE ADJUSTING TOOL

A spiral-balance adjusting tool is designed specifically to adjust a spring under tension. You can buy one from the manufacturer of your windows or from a replacement window company.

A slotted hook on the tool slips over the lower pin on the end of the spiral balance *(right)*. Then you can safely pull down and tilt it out to free the balance from the shoe. Turning the handle clockwise increases tension; counterclockwise decreases it.

e care as you place the baiance back in the shoe. If it lips out, it will shoot up into the tube, possibly causing damage.

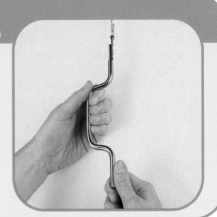

3. REMOVING THE JAMB LINER

• To remove a broken spiral balance on a tilt-in sash, first take off the jamb liner if you find one. To do so, slip a screwdriver under one end of the liner and pry it up so you can grasp the liner and pull it free *(right)*.

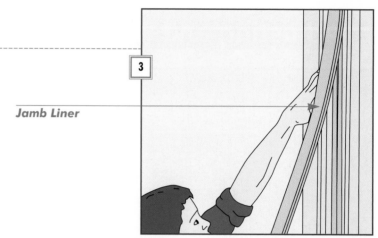

Jamb Liner

4. REPLACING THE SPIRAL BALANCE

• Remove the screw at the top of the spiral balance that secures the tube end to the jamb, and lift out the balance *(right)*.

• Screw an exact replacement to the jamb.

• Rehook the spiral end of the balance into the slot in the shoe with the adjusting tool.

• Adjust the balance as described on page 23, Step 1.

Tube

Block-and-Tackle Balances

1. DETACHING THE CLIP

A block-and-tackle balance is not adjustable. If the window does not open or close properly or does not stay open, you'll need to replace one or more of the balances.

• To remove the lower sash, first flip up the clips at the top of the each sash channel *(right)*.

• If the interior stops hide the clips, remove them and pull up the clips.

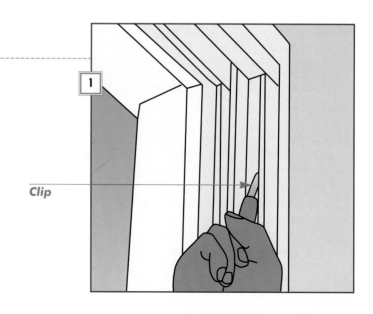

Clip

2

2. REMOVING THE SASHES

• Raise the sash until the clips catch the tops of the balances to disengage them from the sash.

• Push one side of the sash against the jamb and pull the other side out of the frame *(left)*.

• If the upper sash doesn't work properly, lower it and flip up the clips, then take out the sash as described above.

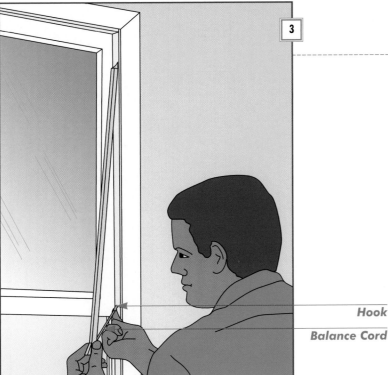

3

Hook

Balance Cord

3. REMOVING THE BALANCE

• Pull the bottom of the balance away from the jamb to expose the balance cord *(left)*.

• Push the hook on the end of the cord up and out of the notch in the jamb, then lift the balance away from the jamb.

• To install a new balance, push the top of the balance under the clip. Hold the balance with one hand while using the other to pull the balance-cord hook and engage it in the notch in the jamb.

FIX IT: Swingers & Sliders

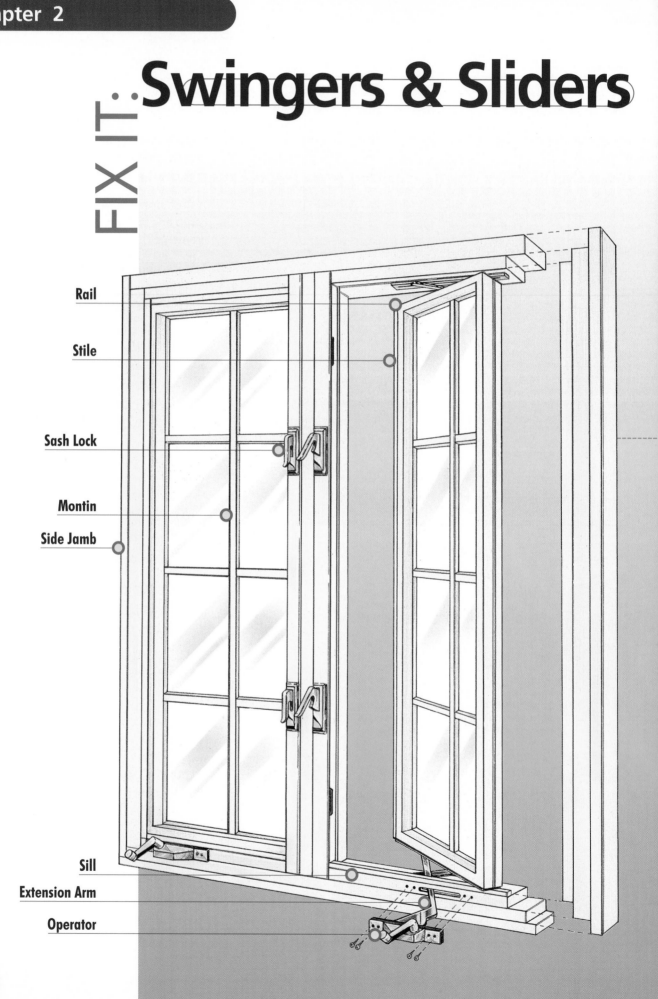

Rail

Stile

Sash Lock

Montin

Side Jamb

Sill

Extension Arm

Operator

Chapter 2

Contents

How They Work

The casement window shown at left is the most common of the swingers, or hinged windows. Other varieties include awning windows—their sashes, called vents, are hinged at the top—hopper windows (hinged at the bottom), and jalousie windows, which have multiple panes hinged at the sides. Sliders, which include patio doors in addition to windows, move side-to-side in tracks, top and bottom.

With the exception of hopper windows, most swingers are opened or closed by turning the handle of an operating mechanism that consists of a set of gears and an extension arm that slides along a track or rod fastened under the sash. Locking systems vary from the front-mounted latches shown here to side-mounted levers built into the sash.

Troubleshooting

Problem	Solution
• **Window doesn't open or close smoothly**	Tighten loose operating mechanism mounting screws **30–33** • Clean and lubricate dirty mechanism (casement **30**; awning **31**; jalousie **30**) • Release jammed extension-arm shoe **30** •
• **Operator handle slips**	Tighten loose handle set screw • Remove handle, clean dirty stem and lubricate **30** • Replace worn gear or operating mechanism (casement **30**; awning **31**; jalousie **33**) •
• **Awning window grinds when opening or closing**	Lubricate faulty linkage; adjust if necessary **32** •
• **Glass slat of jalousie loose or falls out**	Replace broken jalousie clip or rivet **33–34** •
• **Slider doesn't open or close smoothly**	Replace worn glides **35** • Adjust or replace roller assembly **37** • Install steel cap on damaged track **36** •
• **Slider rattles**	Replace worn weather stripping **118** • Replace worn foam insulation **119** • Install steel cap on damaged track **36** • Adjust or replace roller assembly **37** •

Before You Start

If a window opens grudgingly, you may be pleasantly surprised to find that in many instances the only "repair" it needs is a good cleaning and lubrication.

CLEAN IT UP

Scrub away hardened grease on tracks and linkages with a wire brush. You can soak smaller parts such as rollers, glides, and operators in mineral spirits or kerosene. Dry the parts completely and apply white (lithium) grease or spray the parts with a silicone lubricant.

GEARS, GLIDES, LEVERS, AND ROLLERS

Even the best maintenance practices can't keep windows working perfectly forever. Fortunately, parts are easy to repair or replace. Swingers have a tendency to break down more often than other windows because they have so many more moving parts—linkages and gear or lever operators—all of which can wear out. Although sliders put considerable weight on their rollers and track systems, the very simplicity of their mechanisms makes them more dependable than windows with cranks and gears.

Before You StartTips:

⋯▷ To loosen stubborn screws, apply penetrating oil and wait 15 minutes before disassembling.

⋯▷ Have 4- to 6-mil plastic sheeting, 1-by-2s, and 1-1/2-inch common nails on hand to seal a window temporarily in case you run into unexpected problems.

TOOLS

Screwdriver
Electric drill
Utility knife
C-clamps
Cold chisel
Hammer
Pop rivet gun
Pry bar
Wire brush

MATERIALS

Silicone spray lubricant
White (lithium) grease
Weather stripping
Pop rivets

SAFETY FIRST

Wear gloves whenever you work with glass. When removing or installing a patio door, get help from a friend to lift one of these surprisingly heavy doors.

Casement Windows

1. FREEING THE OPERATING MECHANISM

If the mechanism is broken or requires a thorough cleaning, remove it.

● Open the window halfway, then remove the screws holding the operating mechanism to the frame *(right)*. If your window has a lever instead of a crank, take out the screws that attach the pivot mount to the sill.

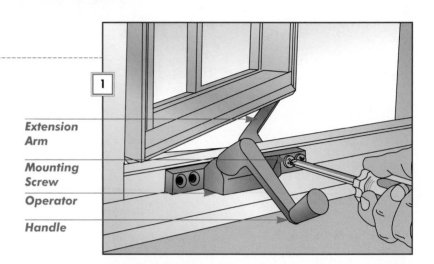

Extension Arm

Mounting Screw

Operator

Handle

2. REMOVING THE EXTENSION-ARM SHOE

● To disengage the extension arm from the sash, slide it along the sash until the extension-arm shoe reaches the access slot.

● Push the extension arm down and pull the shoe through the slot *(right)*. On models without a slot, free the arm by sliding it off the end of the track. If the window is lever-operated, unscrew the pivot plate that secures the lever to the sash.

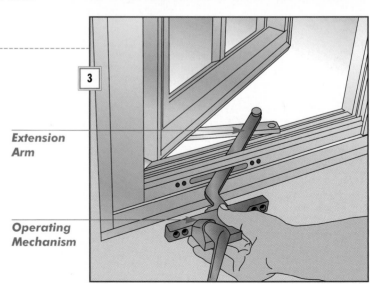

Track

Extension-Arm Shoe

3. REPLACING THE MECHANISM

● Pull the operating mechanism free of its slot in the window frame *(right)*.

● Loosen the handle set screw and remove the handle.

● Examine the interlocking teeth of the handle and operating mechanism. If they or the teeth at the base of the extension arm are rounded or broken, consult a window specialist for replacements.

● To re-install the operator, reverse the steps taken for removal.

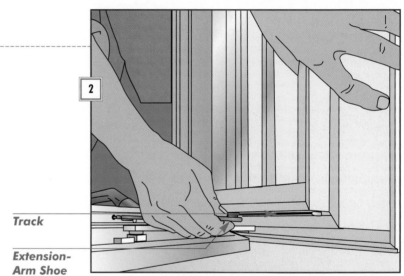

Extension Arm

Operating Mechanism

Single-Awning Windows

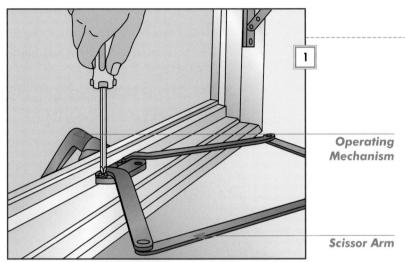

1

Operating
Mechanism

Scissor Arm

Window Sash

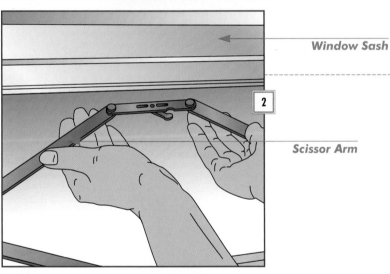

2

Scissor Arm

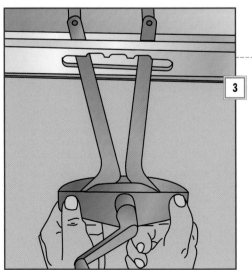

3

1. RELEASING THE MECHANISM

• Open the window as wide as possible.

• Brace the window with blocks of wood so the window won't slam shut when you remove the scissor arms and operator.

• Remove the mounting screws that secure the operating mechanism to the window frame *(left)*.

2. UNHOOKING CLIPS ON THE SASH

• Reach under the sash and unhook the scissor arms from their clips on the sash *(left)*.

• For scissor arms that are screwed to the sash, remove the screws.

• If the window has extension arms that slide along a track on the sash, spread the arms and slide the shoes off each end of the track.

3. REPLACING THE MECHANISM

• Straighten the scissor arms and pull them clear of the window *(left)*.

• If gear or stem splines are rounded or broken, consult a window specialist or the manufacturer for a replacement part.

• To re-install the operating mechanism, straighten the scissor arm and insert it in the frame. Hook the end of the arm onto the window sash, and screw the mechanism to the window frame.

Multiple-Awning Windows

ADJUSTING THE SASH

- To stop a sash from rattling, lower the bracket on each end about 1/16 inch *(right)*.

- For a sash that won't close all the way, raise its bracket 1/16 inch.

- After adjusting a sash, test the window; moving the brackets of one sash affects the operation of the others.

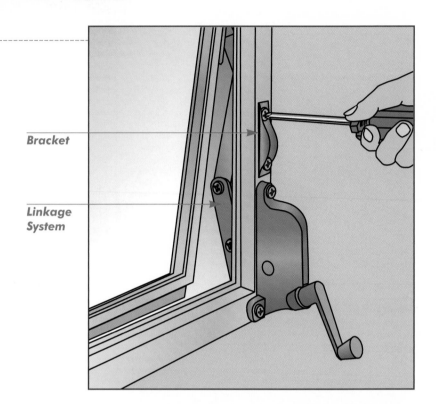

Bracket

Linkage System

REMOVING THE OPERATING MECHANISM

- Unfasten the screws on the front.

- Support the mechanism with one hand while you unscrew the link connecting the gear arm to the linkage system *(inset)*. If you find a stud and snap-on fastener instead of a screw, pry off the fastener, then pull off the stud.

- Pull the operating mechanism from its slot in the window frame.

- If the old mounting screws are stripped, replace them with nuts and bolts *(right)*.

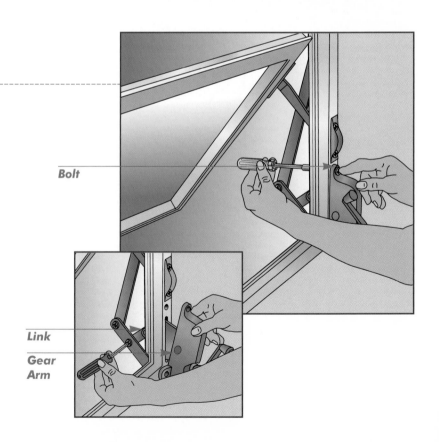

Bolt

Link

Gear Arm

Jalousie Windows

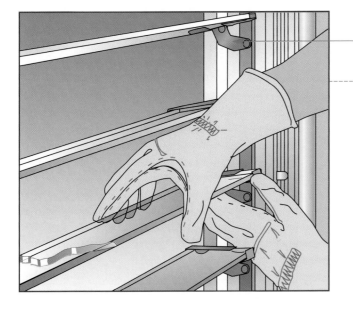

Jalousie Clip

REPLACING A BROKEN PANE

● Wearing heavy work gloves, pull down the lip of the jalousie clip and slide out the cracked or broken glass *(left)*.

● Measure one of the unbroken panes and order a replacement pane cut to size. Have the exposed edges of the new glass rounded for safety.

⚠ **CAUTION:** *Do not bend the lip of the clip more than necessary: It may break.*

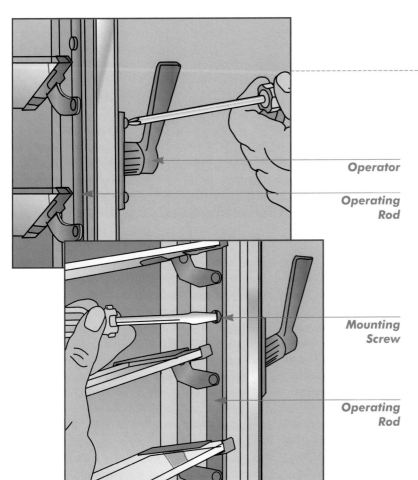

Operator

Operating Rod

Mounting Screw

Operating Rod

REMOVING THE OPERATING MECHANISM

● To remove either a lever operator *(top left)* or a crank operator from a jalousie window, take out its mounting screws.

● Then remove the mounting screw from the operating rod *(bottom left)* and pull out the mechanism. If a stud and a snap-on fastener connect it instead of a screw, pry off the fastener with a screwdriver and then pull out the stud.

● To install the operating mechanism, hold it in place with one hand and re-install the screw that connects the mechanism rod to the operator. Then secure the mechanism to the frame with its mounting screws.

Replacing a Jalousie Clip

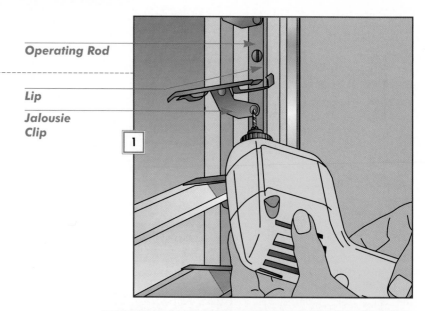

Operating Rod

Lip

Jalousie Clip

1

1. REMOVING A JALOUSIE CLIP

• To replace a broken or worn-out jalousie clip, first remove the glass pane *(page 33).*

• On most jalousie windows, the clips attach to the operating rod and frame via rivets. If this is the case on your window, drill out the rivets with a power drill *(right).* If it has studs instead, pry off the snap-on fasteners with a screwdriver, then pull off the studs. If it has screws, unscrew them.

• Pull out the jalousie clip.

2. INSTALLING A NEW CLIP

• Consult a window specialist or the manufacturer for a replacement clip.

• Position the new clip against the frame and install a new rivet with a pop rivet gun *(below).* To do so, align the holes in the clip and the operating rod, and pop in a new rivet *(right).*

• Gently pull down the lip of the clip, slide the pane into place, and then bend the lip back around the edge of the pane.

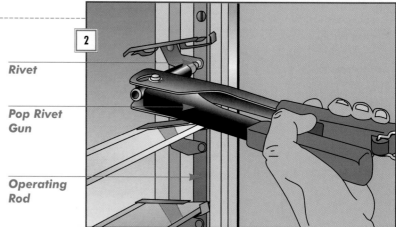

2

Rivet

Pop Rivet Gun

Operating Rod

POP RIVET GUN

One of the handiest tools for repairing moving parts on a modern window is a pop rivet gun *(right).* It's great for replacing the rivets that hold together linkages of metal windows.

Pop rivets are also useful for securing stationary metal parts to each other, like the frame of a metal screen or door.

Rivets are available in various diameters, lengths, and materials (aluminum is common). Choose a rivet that's slightly smaller in diameter than the hole you've drilled. As to length, pick a rivet with a shank about twice as long as the thickness of the materials you'll join, including the thickness of any washers you'll use.

Sliding Windows

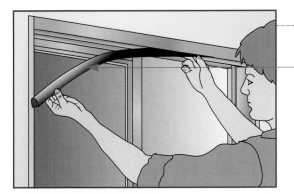

Insulating Foam

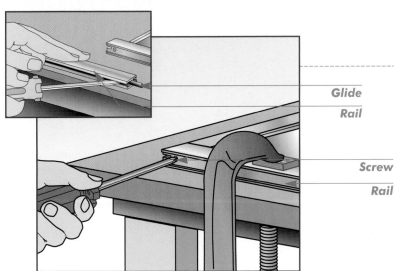

Glide
Rail

Screw
Rail

FIXING A SASH THAT RATTLES

● To replace faulty insulation that can cause rattling, lift up the sash, swing the bottom out, and remove it. Then twist out the liner of the top jamb that holds in the foam.

● Replace the old foam with the same type, but 1/2 inch thicker *(left)*, then snap the liner into place to secure it.

● Set the sash in the top channel, swing in the bottom, then set it into the lower channel.

REPLACING WINDOW GLIDES

● To replace a glide, remove the sash *(above)*.

● Clamp the sash down and remove the screws that secure the stiles to the rails *(left)*. Then knock the bottom rail free with a mallet and a block of wood.

● Insert a screwdriver into the channel in the rail and force out the glide *(inset)*.

● Tap the new glide into the rail with a hammer, and screw the rail to the stile.

Ron's TRADE SECRETS

BURGLAR-PROOFING A SLIDING WINDOW

It's all too easy for an intruder to pry apart the sections of a sliding window or door and shove it open. To prevent this, I secure sliding windows and doors with a dowel, old broomstick, or other piece of wood cut to fit the interior channel *(right)*.

Measure the length of the channel with the window or door closed and locked. With a saw, cut the wood to fit snugly into this space, making sure it lies flat in the channel.

Repairing a Patio Door Track

REMOVING THE PATIO DOOR

• Open the door about halfway. With a helper, lift the door off the rolling surface, pushing it into the top jamb *(right)*. Carefully swing the bottom of the door out.

• Remove the second door in the same way after unscrewing any brackets that secure it.

• Upon completing repairs, re-install the doors: Set the last door you removed in place with the help of friend, and reattach any brackets you removed.

• Then replace the first door by lifting it at an angle, pushing it into the top jamb, and setting it on the rolling surface.

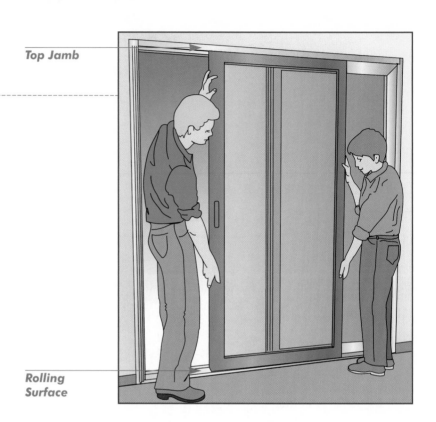

Top Jamb

Rolling Surface

INSTALLING A STEEL CAP

In some cases, you can repair a damaged track by fitting a U-shaped steel cap on top of the old track.

• From a window specialist, buy a cap that's cut to your door's width and that matches your track and fits your door's rollers.

• Invert the cap and snap it onto the rolling surface, pressing down firmly *(right)*.

• Re-install the door. If it binds, adjust the roller assembly *(page 37)*.

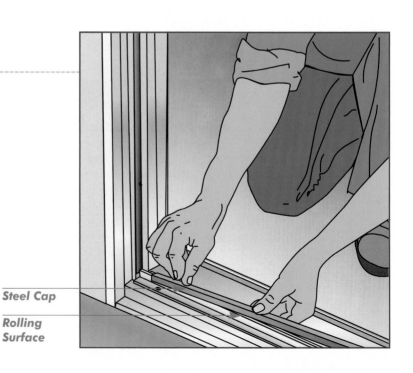

Steel Cap

Rolling Surface

Repairing a Patio Door Roller

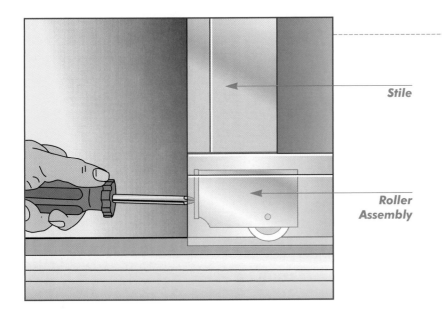

Stile

Roller Assembly

EASING A STICKING DOOR

- When a patio door sticks at the top, find the adjusting screw in the roller assembly in the bottom rail and turn it counterclockwise to lower the door *(left)*.

- If the door sticks at the bottom, enlist a helper to lever the door upward slightly with a utility bar, then turn the screw clockwise.

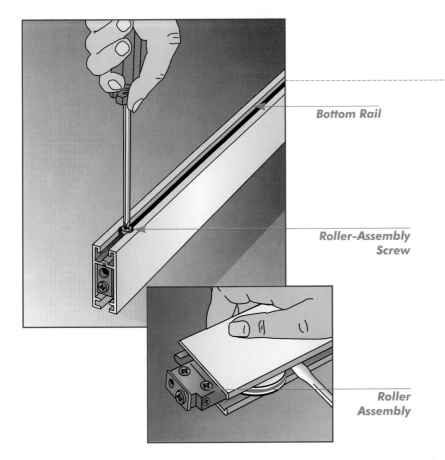

Bottom Rail

Roller-Assembly Screw

Roller Assembly

REPLACING A ROLLER ASSEMBLY

- Take down the door and remove the screws that connect the bottom rail and stiles. Free the rail with a mallet and a block of wood.

- Remove the roller-assembly screw from the top of the bottom rail *(left)*.

- Slide the roller assembly out with a screwdriver *(inset)*. If the roller is damaged, buy a new one.

- Re-install the roller by pushing it into the rail and securing it with a screw.

- To reassemble the door, tap the bottom rail back in place with a mallet. Re-install the screws that secure the bottom rail to the stiles, and rehang the door *(page 36)*.

FIX IT..Doors

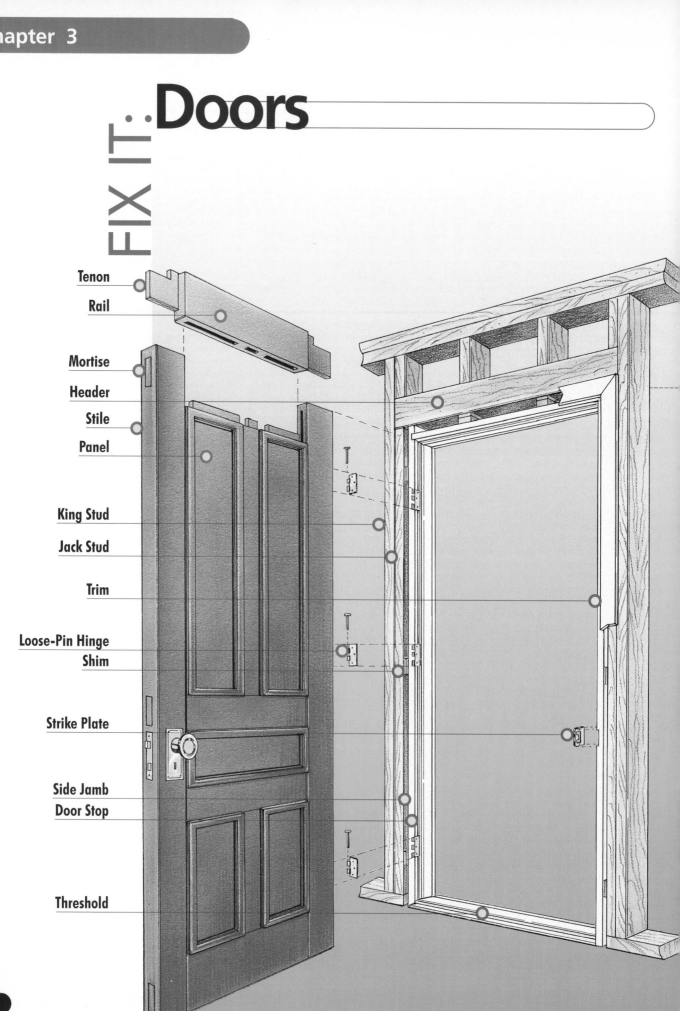

Tenon

Rail

Mortise

Header

Stile

Panel

King Stud

Jack Stud

Trim

Loose-Pin Hinge

Shim

Strike Plate

Side Jamb

Door Stop

Threshold

Chapter 3

Contents

How They Work

Interior and exterior doors come in myriad sizes, shapes, and styles. Solid wood doors commonly grace both the exteriors and interiors of older homes. Most wood doors have frame-and-panel construction; some newer models have a solid wood core covered with a wood veneer.

Inexpensive, hollow-core doors are typically found inside modern homes. Exterior doors are frequently of insulated steel construction and are often designed to look like they're made of wood. Steel doors insulate better than wood doors, and they're stronger and more fire-resistant.

Openings for both interior and exterior doors are framed much alike *(left)*. A header spans the opening and is supported by a pair of jack studs. These in turn attach to king studs that are part of the wall structure. A jamb lines this rough opening to accept the door. Trim covers the space between the jamb and the wall.

Troubleshooting

Problem	Solution
• **Door hinges squeak**	Remove, clean, and oil hinge pins one at a time **46** •
• **Doorknob or handle loose**	Tighten loose set screw **42** • Tighten mounting plate **43** •
• **Door won't close properly**	Clean dirt or paint buildup around latch and lubricate latch **42** • Replace broken latch **43** • Replace broken latch spring **42** • Lubricate stuck latch in interior of lock case **42** • Shim hinges that are set too deep **47** • Adjust strike plate **44** • Shim strike plate to compensate for warped door **47** • Reposition door stop **51** •
• **Door rattles**	Adjust misaligned strike plate **44** • Weather-strip door to compensate for house settling or a door that has shrunk **118** • Shim hinges or strike plate **47–48** • Shim door jamb **52** •
• **Door sticks or binds**	Repair worn hinge screw holes **48** • Determine and correct binding area of warped door **47** •
• **Hole in hollow-core door**	Patch hole **57** •
• **Top-hung sliding door jammed**	Restore rollers to correct position on the track at the top of the doorway **60** • Adjust misaligned bottom guide **60** •
• **Folding door's corner broken off**	Repair corner and reseat pivot pin **58** •
• **Door cracked or splintered**	Repair damaged section **63** • Re-install strike plate **73** • Install reinforcement plate **64** •
• **Door jamb splintered**	Replace damaged section **65** • Re-install strike plate **73** •

Before You Start

TOOLS

As a rule, when a hinged door refuses to open or close as it should, first work on its hinges, then the door, and finally the frame.

COMMON PROBLEMS

You can shim hinges and strike plate *(page 47)* or deepen their mortises *(page 48)*. You can cut doors *(page 54)* or plane them *(page 49)* and shift the jambs in and out *(page 53)*. You repair an exterior door in much the same way as an interior door. But unique to an exterior door is damage due to break-in. In most cases, you can save the door and jamb; however, repair requires careful carpentry *(page 63)*.

Both interior and exterior doors and their jambs are available in wood, steel, or a combination of the two. Steel doors and jambs are rugged and stable and rarely need repair; when they do, the rigid metal offers less of an opportunity for adjustment. For the best of both worlds, many contractors combine a flexible wood jamb, which can be shimmed, with a steel door that's impervious to weather.

Before You Start Tips:

⋯⋗ Before dismounting a door to work on it, make a pair of door jacks *(page 46)*. These simple clamps securely prop up a door so you can work on it safely.

⋯⋗ To keep from losing hinge pins, slip them back into the jamb hinge leaves after you have removed a door.

Electric drill

Utility knife

Chisel

Nail puller

Hammer

C-clamps

Putty knife

Utility or pry bar

Nail set

Locking-grip pliers

Carpenter's square

Handsaw or circular saw

Rubber mallet

Jack and block planes

Adjustable hole saw

MATERIALS

Wood for door jacks

Shims

Wood screws

Spackling compound

Wood putty

Weather stripping

SAFETY FIRST

Wear gloves and safety glasses when doing demolition work. Eye protection is also essential whenever you cut into wood, metal, or plastic with a drill or saw.

Old-Style Knob-and-Latch Assemblies

1. UNSTICKING A LATCH

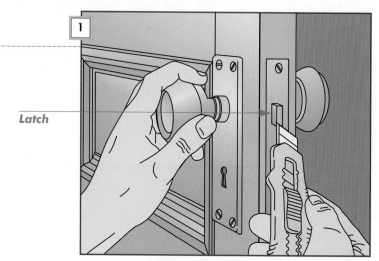

Latch

• Paint buildup is a common cause of a sticking latch. With a utility knife, break the paint seal around the latch and scrape paint off its surface *(right)*.

• If the latch in an old mortise-type lock case continues to stick, remove the lock case for repair or replacement *(Step 2)*.

2. REMOVING A LOCK CASE

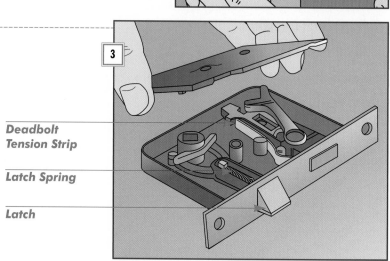

Edge Plate

• Unscrew one of the doorknobs and pull it off its shaft. Then withdraw the shaft from the door by pulling on the other knob.

• With a utility knife, scrape away paint blocking the screw slots at the top and bottom of the lock case edge plate.

• Remove the screws and carefully pry out the case *(right)*.

3. SERVICING THE LOCK CASE

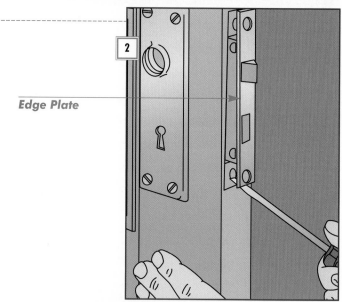

Deadbolt
Tension Strip

Latch Spring

Latch

• With the lock case on a flat surface, unscrew the cover plate and remove it *(right)*. Sketch the interior layout for reference, then spray the works with a silicone lubricant.

• If either the latch spring or deadbolt tension strip is damaged, replace it.

• Check the action on both the latch and the bolt. If either will not budge, enlarge the openings in the lock case with a file, as you would a strike plate *(page 45)*.

Modern Knob-and-Latch Assemblies

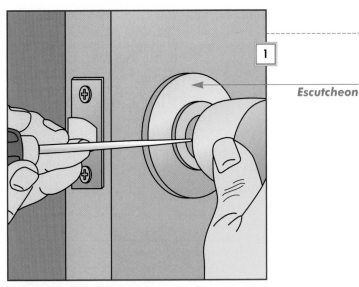

Escutcheon

1. TIGHTENING A KNOB

Sometimes you can secure a loose knob by simply tightening two screws located on the escutcheon. Other types *(left)* require you to remove the doorknob and the escutcheon as follows:

• Turn the knob until the slot on the shank is aligned with the release catch.

• Depress the catch with an awl to release the knob, and pull it free.

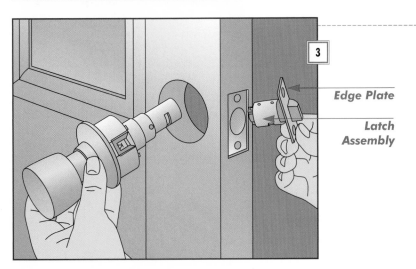

Mounting Plate Screw

Edge Plate Screw

2. TIGHTENING THE MOUNTING PLATE

• Once the knob is removed, twist and pull the escutcheon off the shank.

• Tighten the mounting plate screws to stop the knob assembly from rattling *(left)*.

• If the latch sticks, remove paint buildup *(page 42)*. The latch may be broken if removing paint buildup does not free it; go to Step 3.

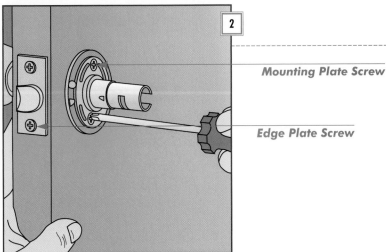

Edge Plate

Latch Assembly

3. REMOVING THE LATCH

• Take out the mounting plate screws and edge plate screws. Then pull gently on the remaining knob, as you wiggle the latch and edge plate free *(left)*. Buy an exact duplicate for the broken latch.

• To reassemble, insert the latch assembly and slide the knob in, wiggling it to engage the latch. Secure the edge and mounting plates with screws. When adding the escutcheon, turn it until it catches. Then set the doorknob on the shank, aligning the catch with the slot, and slide it into place.

Moving a Strike Plate

1. DETERMINING STRIKE PLATE PROBLEMS

• To pinpoint problems with the strike plate, mortise, or latch hole, rub a crayon on the latch edge and close the door *(right)*.

• Open the door and examine the smudge on the strike plate.

• Measure between the smudge and the strike plate opening to find the distance that the strike plate must be shifted to engage the latch. If this distance is less than 1/8 inch, the strike plate can be filed *(Step 6)*; otherwise, go to Step 2.

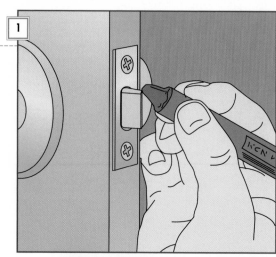

2. MARKING THE JAMB

• Mark the distance on the jamb *(right)*, and extend the mortise to reposition the strike plate *(Step 3)*.

Jamb

Extension Line

Smudge

Strike Plate

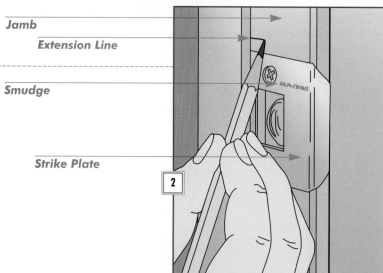

3. EXTENDING THE MORTISE

• Remove the strike plate.

• With a chisel and hammer, cut straight into the jamb at the extension line you marked there, orienting the chisel bevel toward the existing mortise.

• Then with the chisel only, clean out the mortise shape *(right)*.

• Check the fit of the strike plate and then trace the outline of the new strike hole position.

Extension Line

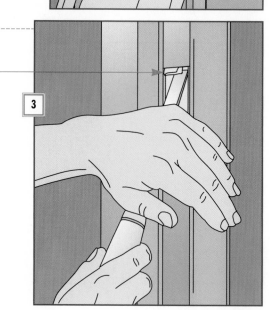

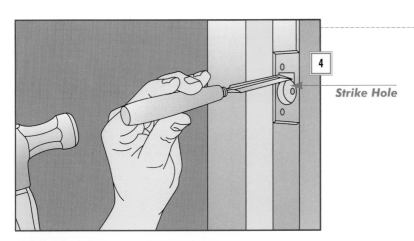

4. ENLARGING THE STRIKE HOLE

• To increase the diameter or depth of a strike hole, chip away wood to the new strike hole outline with a chisel or paring gouge and a hammer *(left)*. Several light cuts will produce a cleaner hole than a few heavy cuts.

Strike Hole

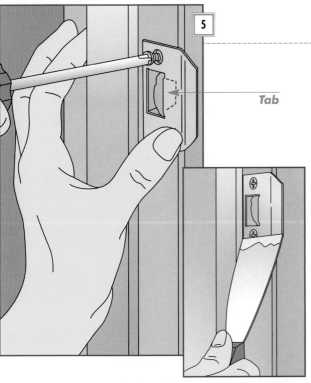

Tab

5. REPOSITIONING THE STRIKE PLATE

• Place the strike plate in position and mark the screw locations. Drill a pilot hole for the top screw, stuffing the old hole with toothpicks if necessary *(page 48)*. Then position the plate and drive the screw *(left)*.

• Next, close the door to make sure the latch slides easily into the hole. If it does, add the bottom screw. If not, adjust the mortise, strike hole, or strike plate *(Step 6)*.

• Fill the gap at the strike plate end with wood putty or spackling compound *(inset)*.

• To silence a rattling door, pry the tab outward with a screwdriver. Push it in slightly if the latch sticks.

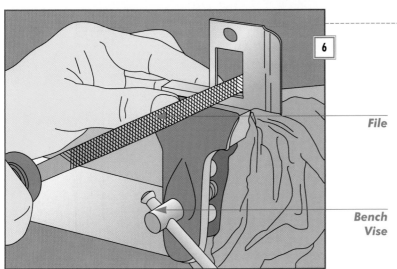

File

Bench Vise

6. FILING THE STRIKE PLATE

• Unscrew the strike plate and clamp it in a bench vise, protecting the plate with cloth.

• With a metal file, file the edge opening to the crayon mark you made in Step 1 *(left)*.

• Then resecure the strike plate with the top screw only. Close the door to see whether the latch catches correctly. If it does, replace the bottom screw. If it does not, you may need to file more.

Dismounting a Door

REMOVING THE DOOR

• Wedge the door open with shims.

• Scrape off any paint that may be binding the hinge pins to the hinge knuckles.

• Beginning with the lowest hinge, tap the hinge pin out with a nail set and a hammer until about 1/2 inch of the pin is exposed *(right).* Then pull the pin out by hand.

• If it will not budge, knock it free with a screwdriver and a hammer *(inset).*

• Then free the middle hinge (if there is one) and top hinge.

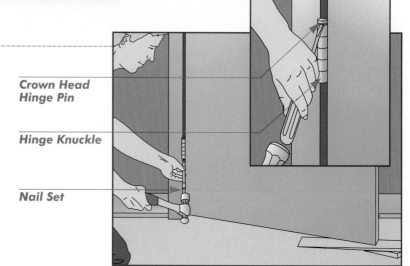

Crown Head Hinge Pin

Hinge Knuckle

Nail Set

PROPPING A DOOR WITH DOOR JACKS

• To work on the edge of a door, make a pair of door jacks *(right),* which use the weight of the door to clamp it upright. Each jack requires an 18-inch strip of 1/4-inch plywood with two scraps nailed to the bottom as feet and two scraps of 2-by-4 nailed to the top, 2 inches apart.

Door Jack

Ron's TRADE SECRETS

DEALING WITH STUBBORN HINGE PINS
Hinge pins can be difficult to remove because of built-up grease and dirt in the hinge barrel. Before you remount a door, spray a small brass wire brush (like the kind used to clean guns) with mineral spirits and run it in and out of the hinge barrel. Then to prevent future problems, file a small V-notch in the hinge knuckle directly below the head of the pin *(right).* The notch allows you to slip a screwdriver under the head to drive the pin out with a hammer.

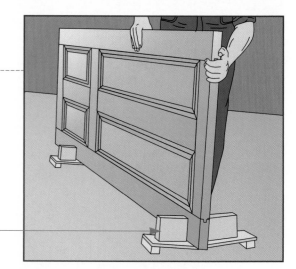

Causes of Binding

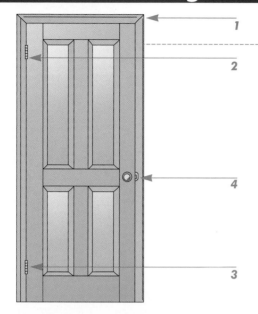

CORRECTING A BINDING DOOR

When rubbing occurs along the length of a door's latch edge, deepen all the hinge mortises *(page 48),* or plane the full length of the hinge edge *(page 49).* If the latch edge rubs only near the top *(1),* deepen the mortise of the corresponding hinge *(2).* If the top edge binds, shim the same hinge or deepen the mortise of the lowest hinge *(3).* The same technique works for a door that rubs near the bottom. If binding occurs at the latch area *(4),* deepen the strike plate mortise *(page 45).*

How to Shim Hinges

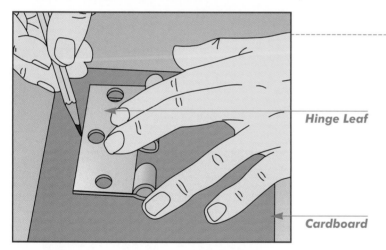

Hinge Leaf

Cardboard

Full Shim

MAKING THE SHIM

● Remove the pin of the hinge that needs shimming *(page 46).* Then unscrew the jamb hinge leaf.

● Trace the leaf and its screw holes on a piece of thin cardboard *(left),* then cut out the pattern you've traced. For fine adjustments, cut out one-third of the traced pattern to make a partial shim *(Step 3).*

● Use an awl to puncture the cardboard at each screw location.

SHIMMING THE FULL HINGE

● Repin the hinge leaf and place one or more shims in the hinge mortise *(left).*

● Position the hinge leaf over the shims and secure it with hinge screws.

● If the screw holes are too large, pack them with toothpicks *(page 48).*

● Then test whether the door closes smoothly. Add or remove shims as needed.

SHIMMING WITH A PARTIAL SHIM

Placed behind the pin edge of the hinge leaf, a partial shim will make the door swing slightly farther into the jamb; placed behind the outer edge of the hinge leaf, it will pull the door slightly away from the door stop.

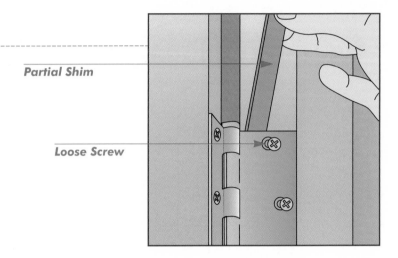

Partial Shim

Loose Screw

● To install a partial shim, loosen the hinge leaf screws and slide the shim behind the leaf *(right);* use shims on both the top and bottom hinges.

Deepening a Hinge Mortise

1. ETCHING THE MORTISE DEPTH

● To work on the jamb mortise alone, wedge the door open. If deepening the door mortise, dismount the door and set it in door jacks *(page 46).* Split a change in mortise depth of 1/8 inch or more between both mortises.

● Unscrew the hinge leaf from the mortise you plan to deepen, and score the perimeter of the mortise with a utility knife *(right).*

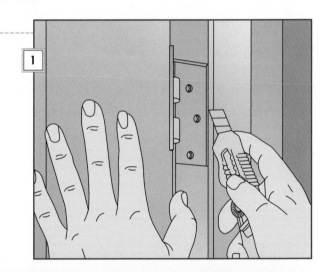

1

Ron's TRADE SECRETS

TIGHTENING SCREWS WITH TOOTHPICKS
Quite often a door will bind simply because its hinges are loose. Over time, the weight and daily use of the door combine to pull the screws out of the jamb. In some cases, a longer screw will save the day. Or you can give the old screws something to grip. I always carry a box of round toothpicks in my toolbox for just this purpose. Simply push a few toothpicks into the hole, and snap them off flush *(right).* No glue is needed; re-installing the screws will wedge the toothpicks tight. This technique is also useful when you need to shift a screw hole slightly, such as when repositioning a strike plate.

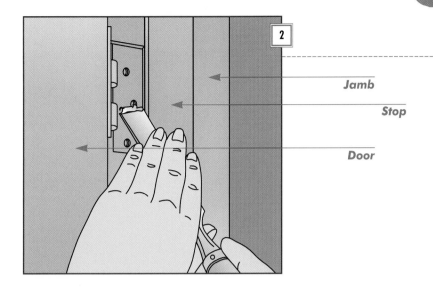

2. CHISELING THE MORTISE

- Holding a wood chisel with the beveled edge facing the mortise, and working from the center of the depression toward the perimeter, clean out the mortise to the required depth *(left)*. Use hand force only.

- Place the hinge leaf in the mortise, making sure that it doesn't rock. If you made the mortise too deep, shim it *(page 47)*.

- Reattach the hinge leaf.

Planing a Door to Shape

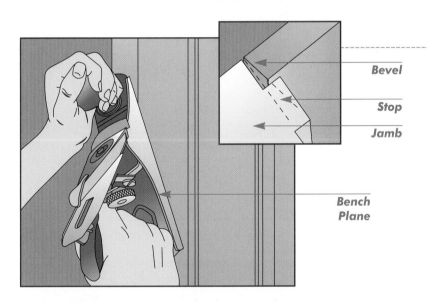

SPOT-PLANING A DOOR

- To spot-plane, first wedge the door open with shims.

- Set the blade on a bench plane for a light cut, and test it on a scrap of wood.

- Take off just enough wood so the edge will not catch on the jamb as the door is closed *(left)*.

- The latch edge of a door is beveled so it can swing close *(inset)*; if you smooth off the bevel, reshape it with the plane or with sandpaper.

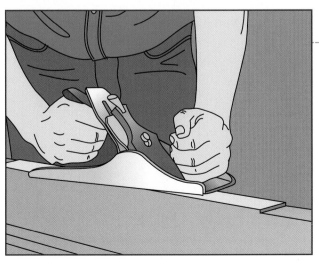

PLANING THE ENTIRE EDGE

- Remove the door and its hinges and prop it securely, latch side down *(page 46)*.

- With a bench plane set for a light cut, plane the entire length of the door *(left)*; the long base of the plane will help you produce a straight, flat surface.

- If you shave so much wood from the hinge side that the hinge mortises become too shallow, pause and deepen the mortises *(page 48)*.

PLANING DOOR TOPS AND BOTTOMS

If more than 1/4 inch of the door end needs to be removed, cut it *(page 54)* rather than planing it.

● Spot-plane the top of the door with the door still hung; to plane the door bottom, remove it and prop it securely *(page 46)*.

● Set the bench plane for a light cut and plane the door, making sure to go in the direction of the grain *(right)*. To avoid splintering, lift the plane before you reach the end grain of the stiles.

Bench Plane

A BLOCK PLANE FOR THE STILES

● Plane the end grain of a stile with a block plane and a freshly sharpened blade set for an extremely light cut *(right)*.

● The lower angle of a block plane's blade allows it to cleanly shear off the stubborn end grain.

● Shave in short, light strokes, from the corner inward.

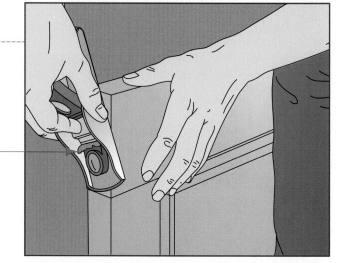

Block Plane

Ron's TRADE SECRETS

SUPPORTING A PLANE WITH 2-BY-4S

Planing a door edge flat and square can be difficult even for an experienced woodworker. A trick I've learned is to clamp a couple of straight 2-by-4s parallel to the door edge as an aid in holding the plane at right angles to the edge *(right)*. If you attach the boards below the edge, they act as a depth gauge; stop work as soon as the plane begins to cut into the 2-by-4s. The guides also allow you to skew the plane as shown in the photograph. This technique produces a shearing cut, which severs wood fibers cleanly and lessens the chance that the plane will tear the wood.

Repositioning the Door Stop

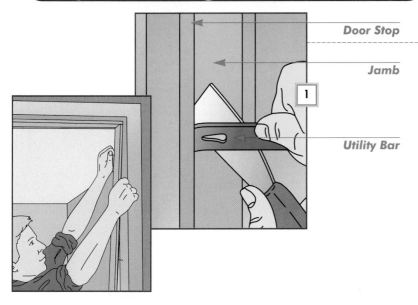

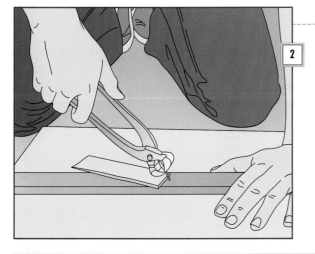

Door Stop

Jamb

Utility Bar

1. REMOVING THE STOP

● Score any paint sealing the stop to the jamb with a utility knife.

● Starting at the top of the doorway, insert a putty knife between the stop and the jamb. Tap the knife gently to open a crack between the stop and the jamb.

● Next, slip a utility bar into the crack, pivoting it on the blade to protect the wood *(left)*. Exert gentle pressure, lifting the stop out about 1/4 inch at each nail.

● Slip the utility bar behind the stop and use both hands to pull the stop free *(inset)*.

2. REMOVING NAILS IN THE STOP/JAMB

● Pull out old nails from a door stop you plan to reuse. Use a nail puller to grip their shanks where they protrude from the back of the stop, rolling the tool's head against a shim to protect the wood *(left)*.

● Remove any nails left in the jamb.

● If you broke the door stop when you removed the nails, take the pieces to a lumberyard for an exact replacement.

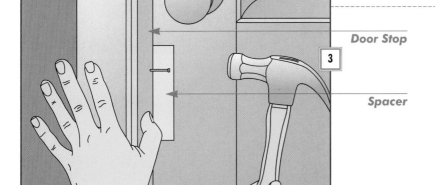

Door Stop

Spacer

3. REPOSITIONING/SECURING THE STOP

● Close the door, and position the stop and a thin cardboard spacer against it near the latch.

● Lightly press the stop against the cardboard and drive a finishing nail, slightly larger than the ones you removed, into the closest nail hole *(left)*. Leave the nail 1/8 inch proud.

● Continue driving nails, alternately nailing above and below the latch. Doing so forces the stop to conform to the door.

4. SETTING/FILLING NAIL HOLES

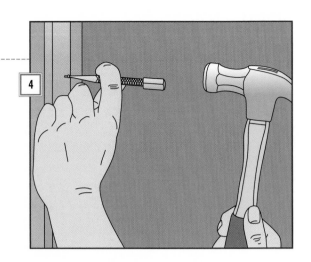

- With the stop in place, check to see that the door rests evenly against it.

- Then set the nails 1/16 inch below the surface with a hammer and a nail set *(right)*.

- If the wood is to be painted, fill the set-nail holes with spackling compound. For wood that is to be stained, use wood putty.

How to Shim a Door Jamb

1. REMOVING THE TRIM

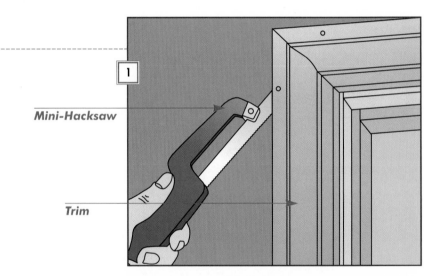

- If a door does not overlap the door stop, first remove the stop *(page 51)*.

- Sever any built-up paint seal between the trim and the wall with a utility knife, then cut the nails holding the trim to the wall with a mini-hacksaw *(right)*.

- Pry the trim away from the jamb, as you did for the stop, and remove the nails.

Mini-Hacksaw

Trim

2. SHIMMING THE JAMB

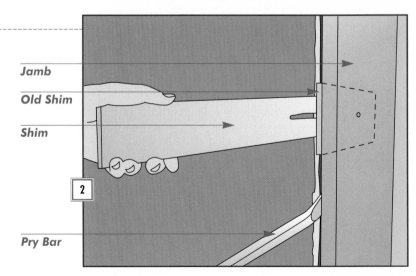

- Cut a notch at the thin end of a shim.

- Insert a pry bar between the jamb and jack stud, and lift the jamb out so you can see the shank of the shim nail.

- Fit the notched end of the shim around the nail *(right),* and close the door.

- If the gap between the door edge and jamb is 1/8 inch or less, drive a nail through the jamb to secure the new shim and re-install the trim. For gaps wider than 1/8 inch, continue to add shims as needed.

Jamb

Old Shim

Shim

Pry Bar

Straightening a Bowed Jamb

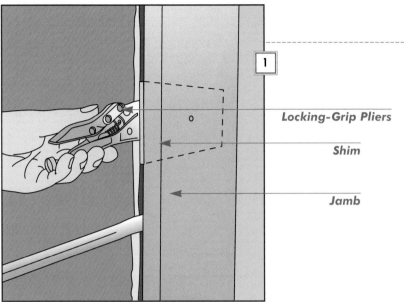

Locking-Grip Pliers

Shim

Jamb

1. PRYING OUT THE JAMB

• Hold a long, straight 2-by-4 against the jamb and mark the high point of the bow.

• If the bow is slight, reseat the jamb by striking a 2-by-4 held against the high point with a mallet.

• If that does not work, remove some shims by first prying off the stop *(page 51)* and trim *(page 52)*.

• With a pry bar, lever the jamb outward far enough to fix locking-grip pliers near the tip of the nail passing through the shims *(left)*.

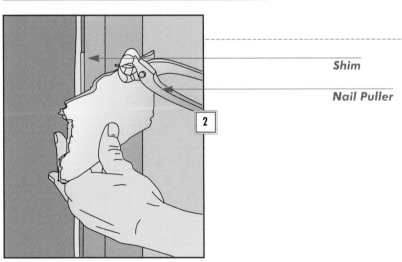

Shim

Nail Puller

2. PULLING OUT NAILS

• Push the jamb in so the nail head protrudes.

• Protect the jamb with a thin scrap of wood, and pull the nail out with a nail puller just enough for one of the shims behind the jamb to fall free *(left)*.

• Push the jamb against the shims to check whether it is straight. If not, free another shim and recheck. Restore shims *(page 52)* if too many fall out. Once the jamb is straight, drive the shim nail back into the jamb.

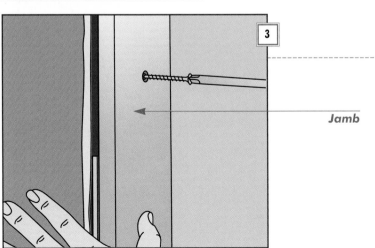

Jamb

3. DRAWING IN THE JAMB

• Drill a countersunk shank hole for a 3-inch screw through the high point of the bowed jamb and a pilot hole into the jack stud behind it.

• Drive in the screw until it pulls the jamb straight *(left)*.

• Then cover the screw head with wood putty or spackling compound and replace the trim and door stop.

Tightening a Door Joint

1. DRILLING A LAG SCREW HOLE

• Remove the door and prop it with door jacks *(page 46)*.

• Drill a 3/4-inch cavity to accept the head of a lag screw *(right)*.

• Then with a bit 1/16 inch smaller than the lag screw shank, drill through the stile and into the rail.

• Finally, to prevent the shank from binding, rebore the hole in the stile with a bit slightly larger than the screw shank.

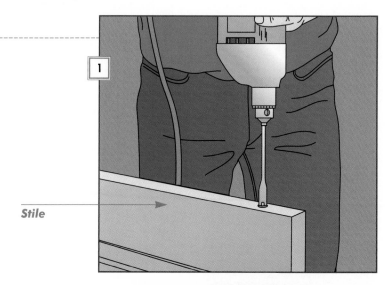

Stile

2. SCREWING THE PIECES TOGETHER

• Clean the gap between the rail and stile with a putty knife.

• Tighten the screw gradually with a socket wrench *(right)*, perhaps only a few turns each day.

• Just before the joint closes, inject carpenter's glue between the stile and rail.

• Then fill the hole with wood putty or spackling compound, and sand smooth.

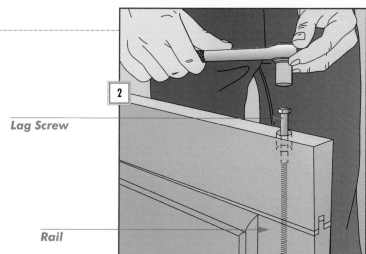

Lag Screw

Rail

Trimming a Solid Door

1. MEASURING AND MARKING

• Remove the door from its hinges *(page 46)* and lay it flat on sawhorses.

• Draw a line along a carpenter's square to shorten the door as required *(right)*. Extend the line across the door.

 CAUTION: *Always leave at least 3 inches of rail to maintain the door's structural integrity.*

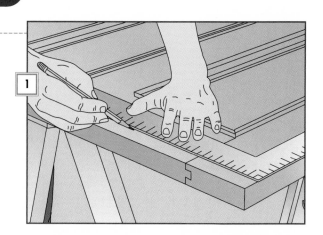

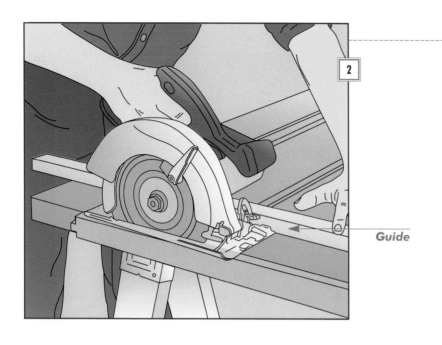

Guide

2. CUTTING THE DOOR

• Adjust the cutting depth of a circular saw blade to 1/4 inch deeper than the thickness of the door.

• Clamp a piece of wood to the door as a guide for the base plate of the saw to ensure a straight cut. Wearing protective eyewear, trim off the waste *(left)*.

• After cutting, smooth any roughness or splinters with sandpaper wrapped around a sanding block.

• Hang the door *(page 46)*.

• If necessary, make any minor adjustments with a plane *(page 49)*.

Cutting a Hollow-Core Door

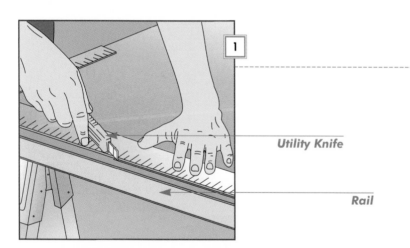

Utility Knife

Rail

1. MINIMIZING SPLINTERS

• Mark the door for trimming as you would a solid door, then score through the veneer with a utility knife *(left)*.

• If the knife did not encounter the underlying rail, score through the veneer on the other side as well.

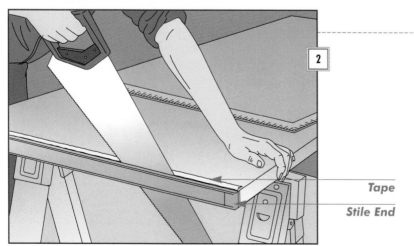

Tape

Stile End

2. MAKING THE CUT

• Run a strip of masking tape along the line to prevent the saw teeth from catching and splintering the veneer as you saw the door.

• Trim the door with a handsaw *(left)*, or a circular saw and guide *(above)*. Cut along the waste side of the line scored in Step 1.

• If you have cut the entire rail from the door, proceed to Step 3. Otherwise, smooth the edge with sandpaper and a sanding block, then rehang the door.

3. FREEING THE RAIL

• Run the blade of a putty knife between the rail and the veneer to break the glue seal *(right)*.

• Snap off the stile ends and scrape away splintered veneer and dried adhesive with a putty knife or paint scraper.

• Drive a short finishing nail partway into the rail near each end to aid in repositioning it *(Step 5)*.

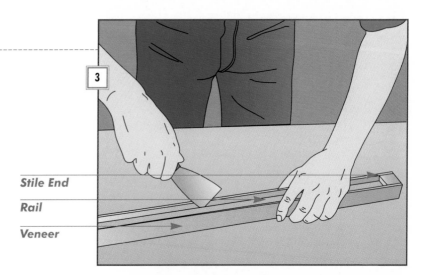

Stile End
Rail
Veneer

4. GLUING THE RAIL

• Push back any support material inside the door that might interfere with insertion of the rail.

• Apply a thin bead of carpenter's glue to both veneer panels, just inside the opening. Allow the glue to set for a few minutes, until it becomes tacky.

• Then insert the rail in the door *(right)*.

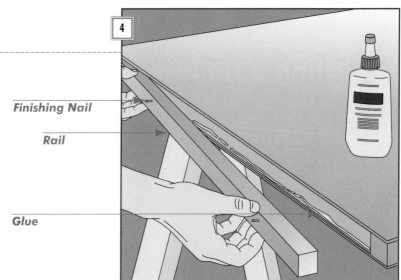

Finishing Nail
Rail
Glue

5. CLAMPING THE RAIL

• Lightly tap the rail into position with a rubber mallet. If you accidentally tap either end in too far, pull on the finishing nails to adjust it.

• Then with C-clamps and strips of wood to protect the veneer, clamp the veneer against the rail *(right)*.

• When the glue is dry, remove the clamps and pull out the nails.

• Hang the door.

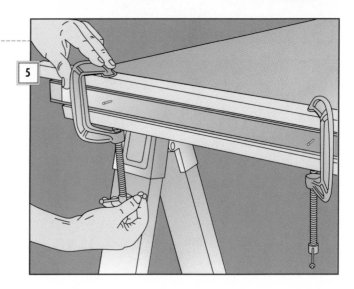

A Patch for a Hollow-Core Door

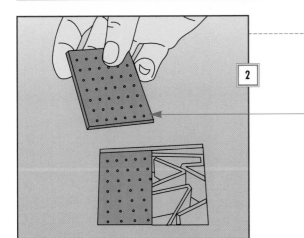

Damaged Area

Veneer

1. CUTTING OUT THE DAMAGE

• With a sharp utility knife, cut out a rectangle around the damaged area in the veneer *(left)*.

• Trim away splinters and push the support materials inside away from the hole.

2. ADDING CARDBOARD INSERTS

• Cut strips of cardboard 1/16 inch narrower than the depth of the hole. Fold the strips loosely and insert them in the hole.

• Cut a rectangle of the same material 1/2 inch larger than the hole. Perforate this piece with an awl and then cut it in half. Insert one half into the hole, then slip the other piece in *(left)*.

• Apply spackling compound. When dry, sand it smooth. Then paint the door.

Perforated Cardboard

Ron's TRADE SECRETS

FILLING A HOLE WITH EXPANDING FOAM

As an alternative to filling a hole in a hollow-core door with strips of cardboard, I use expanding foam *(right)*. First I remove any splinters, but I don't cut out the damaged area until the foam has cured overnight. After it has cured, I also trim away excess foam to leave a depression for spackling compound. When the spackling compound has dried, I sand and paint the door.

A couple of pointers when using expanding foam. First, always wear gloves and provide adequate ventilation. Second, fill the cavity no more than two-thirds full to allow for expansion.

Folding Doors

CORRECTING A DRAGGING DOOR

• Fold the door open and lift it out of the floor bracket, then pull it down and out of the slider and top corner bracket *(right)*.

• To prevent the door from dragging—on newly installed carpeting, for example— raise the floor bracket. To do so, unscrew it and trace its outline on a scrap of wood no thicker than the distance between the top of the door and the slider.

• Cut out the shape and insert it as a shim under the floor bracket *(lower inset)*. Re-install the bracket using longer screws.

• To rehang the door, fit the top corner pin into its bracket, then lift the door and set the pin on the bottom of the door into the floor bracket.

• Next, depress the spring-pivot pin on top of the door, slip it into the slider, then release it *(upper inset)*.

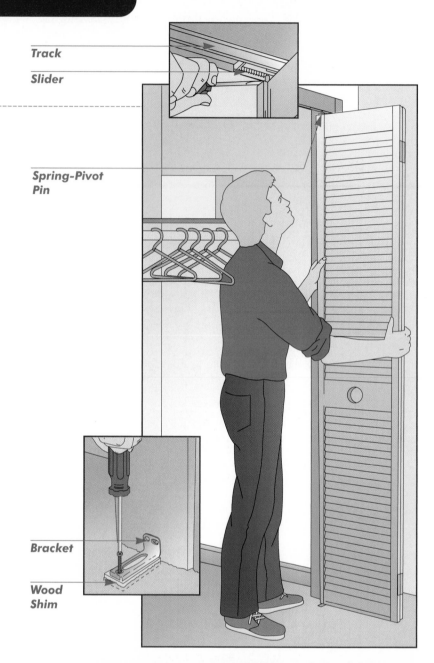

Track

Slider

Spring-Pivot Pin

Bracket

Wood Shim

REPAIRING A BROKEN CORNER

• Remove the door *(above)* and place it on sawhorses.

• Apply a small amount of glue to the broken piece, fit it in place, and secure it with a pipe clamp padded with wooden shims.

• Before the glue sets, tap the pin in place with a screwdriver and a mallet *(right)*. Remove the clamps after the glue has dried.

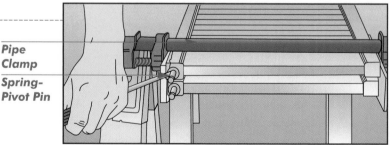

Pipe Clamp

Spring-Pivot Pin

Replacing a Louver

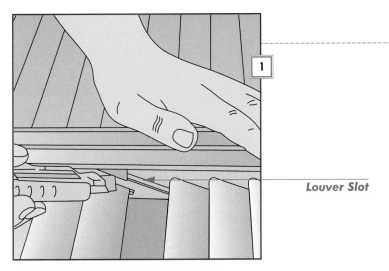

Louver Slot

1. EXTENDING THE SLOT

• Remove the door *(page 58)* and place it on sawhorses.

• Pull out any pieces of broken louver that may still be attached.

• Working on the back of the door, score a notch at the louver slot on each side of the door panel with a utility knife *(left)*.

2. REMOVING THE WASTE

• With a sharp wood chisel and a hammer, carefully cut out each notch as a single piece, extending the louver slot to the edge of the door stile *(left)*.

• Keep the pieces you cut out for replacement after you fit the new louver.

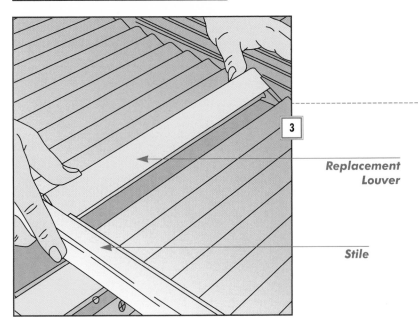

Replacement
Louver

Stile

3. INSTALLING THE NEW LOUVER

• Buy a new louver of the same width as the others. Measure the distance between the stiles of the door, and add 1/8 inch.

• With a handsaw and miter box, cut the new louver to size.

• Stain or paint it to match the other louvers and push it into the slots *(left)*.

• Glue the chiseled pieces in place and rehang the door *(page 58)*.

Top-Hung Sliding Doors

RETRACKING A TOP-HUNG DOOR

• To fix a door that has jumped its track at the top of the doorway, first remove the bottom guide from the floor.

• Check inside the closet to see whether the track has access slots to permit re-insertion of the rollers.

• Swing the door out and lift it upward *(right)*. If the track has access slots, fit the rollers through the slots and into the track. For a door without access slots, set the rollers on top of the track.

ADJUSTING THE BOTTOM GUIDE

• Sliding doors also jam because the bottom guide becomes askew. If this happens, loosen the screws in the guide, realign it, and retighten the screws.

• If a door slips out of the guide, it may be necessary to fit a wood shim under the guide to raise it *(right)*.

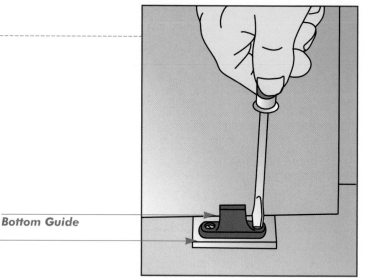

Bottom Guide

Shim

CORRECTING A DRAGGING DOOR

• Some sliding doors have adjustable roller brackets that allow you to raise the door, say, to accommodate new carpeting. To increase door height, loosen the adjusting screws *(right)*, raise the door, and retighten the screws.

• If the door needs to be raised more than the adjustment allows, or if your door isn't adjustable, remove the door and cut the bottom *(page 54)* or plane it *(page 49)*.

• To compensate for raising the door, add shims under the bottom guide *(above)*.

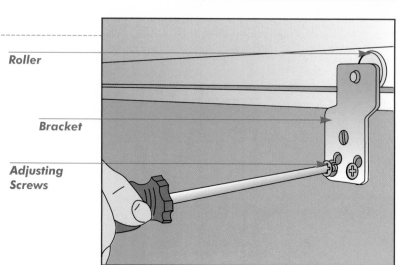

Roller

Bracket

Adjusting
Screws

A New Door Sill

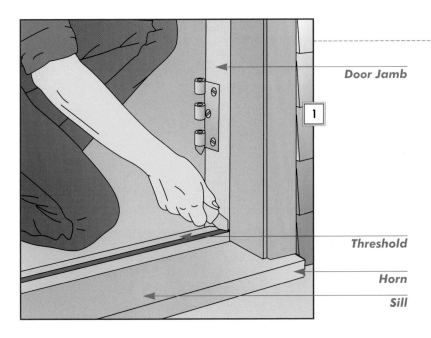

Door Jamb

Threshold

Horn

Sill

1. GETTING AT THE SILL

• Use a utility knife to cut away any caulk around the door jamb *(left)*.

• Remove the wood or metal threshold *(page 122)*.

• If you can see where the sill ends, measure the length of the sill, indoors and out; the difference is the combined length of the sill horns.

• Otherwise, measure the sill after you have removed it *(Step 4)*.

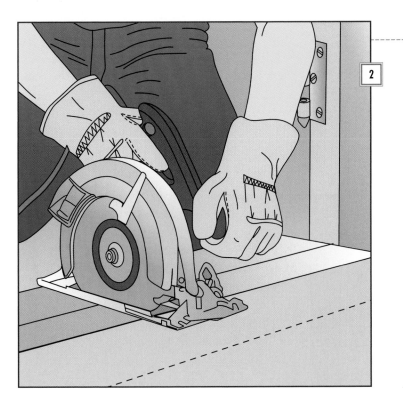

2. CUTTING THE SILL

If the sill is badly rotted, break it away in small pieces with a cold chisel and hammer. Cut less-damaged sills with a circular saw *(left)*. To do so:

• Fit the saw with an old combination blade. Set the saw to cut 1/8 inch shallower than the thickness of the sill.

• Wearing goggles and work gloves, cut through the middle of the sill, perpendicular to the wood grain *(left)*.

3. Prying up the sill

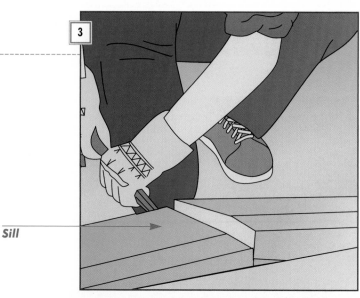

- Free the sill by forcing a pry bar under the cut. Lever up the sill just enough to loosen it from the jamb nails *(right)*.

- Pull out each half of the sill sideways from under the jamb. Snap off any protruding nails in the jamb *(page 16)*.

- Try closing the door; if it does not close, the jambs have bowed and need to be straightened *(page 53)*.

 CAUTION: *Too much prying force could damage the jamb.*

Sill

4. Installing the new sill

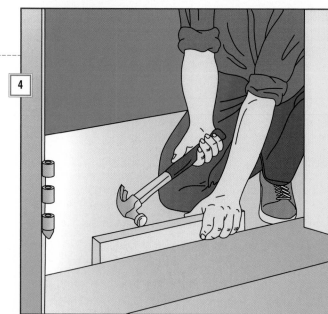

- Mark and cut a new hardwood door sill as for a window *(page 16, Step 4)*. Apply a finish to the sill.

- Clean the sill opening and insert the ends of the new sill under the edges of the jambs.

- Protecting the sill's finish with scrap wood, tap the sill into place with a hammer *(right),* working from the center of the sill out to the jambs.

5. Toenailing the sill

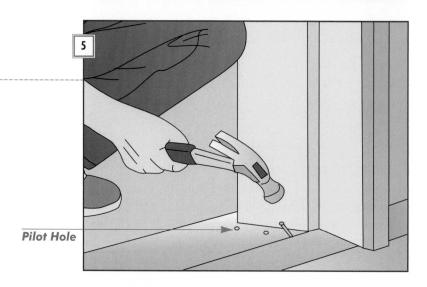

- Drill pilot holes at each end of the sill, angled toward the jamb.

- Then toenail the sill to the jamb with finishing nails *(right)*.

Pilot Hole

Restoring a Door after a Break-In

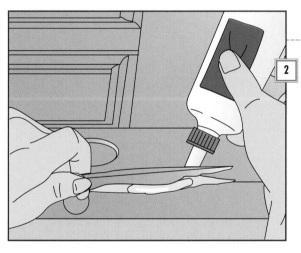

1. ASSESSING BREAK-IN DAMAGE

- Remove the locks *(left)*. If the deadbolt or lockset is broken, repair it *(page 68)* or buy a new one.

- Check the door for cracks and splinters and repair them *(Step 2)*.

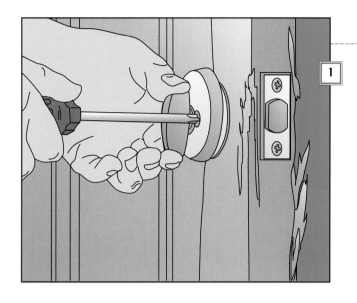

2. APPLYING GLUE TO SPLINTERS

- Squeeze a generous amount of carpenter's glue around the splinters and into the cracks *(left)*. Lift the splintered sections gently to prevent them from snapping off.

- Fit broken pieces back into place.

- Use masking tape to secure small splinters.

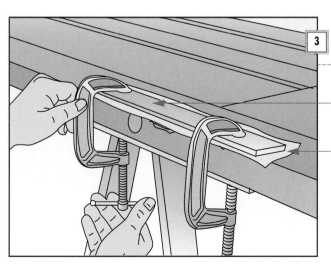

Wood
Scrap

Waxed
Paper

3. CLAMPING SPLINTERS AND CRACKS

- Cover the glued area with waxed paper, and use C-clamps and wood scraps to clamp the repair *(left)*.

- To repair a deep crack along the grain, insert a utility bar, spread the crack slightly to fill it with carpenter's glue, and use a pipe clamp to close the crack. Allow the repair to set overnight, then remove any excess glue with a putty knife or chisel.

4. PLUGGING A LOCK HOLE

• Clamp a piece of wood about 1/8 inch thicker than the door to a workbench, and use an adjustable hole saw *(inset)* to cut a plug to fit the hole in the door.

• Cut a length of 1/4-inch dowel to match the plug's thickness. Coat the dowel with carpenter's glue and tap it into the plug's center hole. Then coat the side of the plug with carpenter's glue and tap it into the hole *(right)*.

• Let the glue dry overnight and level the plug with a plane or sandpaper.

• Refinish or repaint the door.

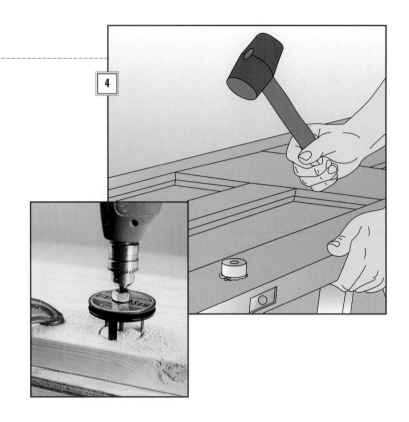

5. INSTALLING A REINFORCEMENT PLATE

To help thwart future break-ins, consider adding a steel reinforcement plate that slips over the door's edge.

• Position the plate on the door and mark its top and bottom on the door's edge. With a wood chisel, cut a mortise in the edge of the door to accommodate the thickness of the plate.

• Reposition the plate and mark the holes for the deadbolt cylinder and bolt *(page 71)*. Remove the plate and drill the holes.

• Then cut the mortise for the deadbolt, install the edge plate *(page 72)*, and screw the reinforcement plate over it *(right)*.

• Install the deadbolt cylinder.

Reinforcement Plate

Repairing a Splintered Jamb

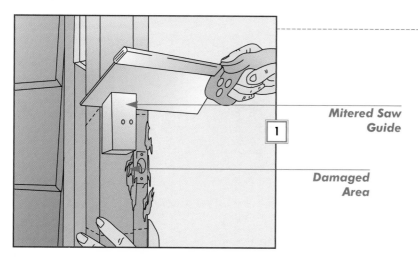

Mitered Saw Guide

Damaged Area

1. REMOVING THE DAMAGED SECTION

- After removing the trim *(page 52)* and strike plate, mark horizontal lines above and below the damaged section.

- In a miter box, cut a block of wood at 45 degrees and nail it to the jamb as a saw guide. (Cutting the jamb at an angle helps hide the patch.)

- Saw through the door stop and jamb *(left)*, then turn the guide over and make similar cuts at the lower line.

- Remove the pieces as well as any nails.

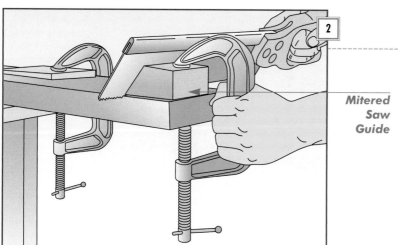

Mitered Saw Guide

2. CUTTING A PATCH

- Buy wood the same type, width, and thickness as the jamb and the stop.

- Mark the length of the patch on the jamb piece and use the saw guide to cut it to length at opposite angles *(left)*.

- Then cut a patch for the stop as you did for the jamb.

- Test the fit of both pieces and trim them as needed.

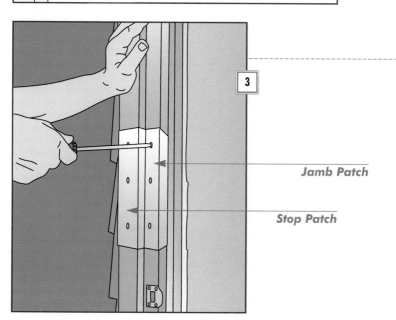

Jamb Patch

Stop Patch

3. SPLICING THE PATCH

- With the jamb and stop patches in place, drill countersunk pilot holes for screws. Space the holes at 4-inch intervals, 1 inch from the edge.

- Coat the edges of the patches with carpenter's glue and screw them in place *(left)*.

- When the glue is dry, smooth the patch with sandpaper. Cover the screw heads with wood putty.

CAUTION: *Do not drill a hole where the deadbolt will be installed.*

FIX IT: Door Locks

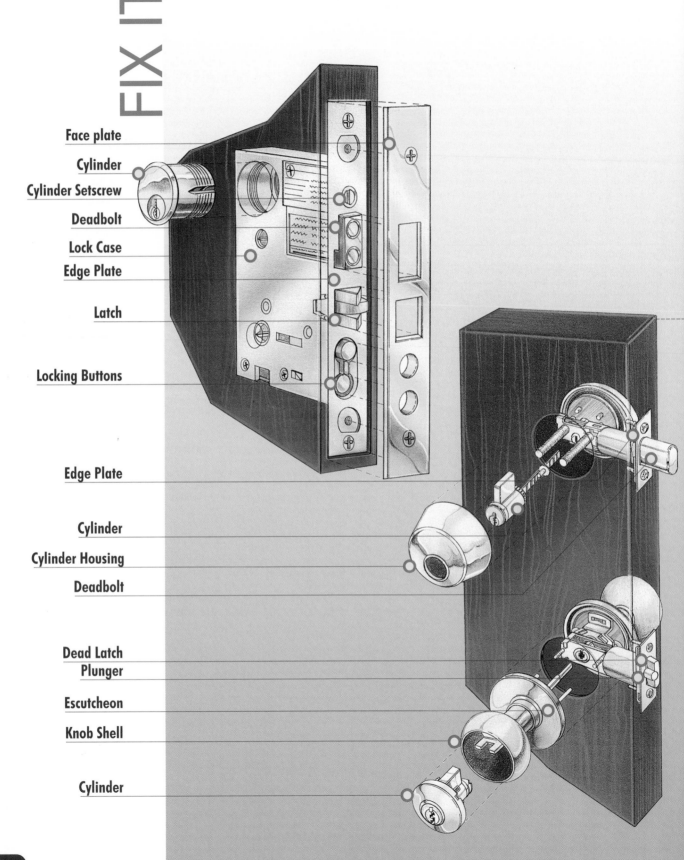

Face plate

Cylinder

Cylinder Setscrew

Deadbolt

Lock Case

Edge Plate

Latch

Locking Buttons

Edge Plate

Cylinder

Cylinder Housing

Deadbolt

Dead Latch
Plunger

Escutcheon

Knob Shell

Cylinder

Chapter 4

Contents

How They Work

Doors of modern homes are typically secured with two separate locks: a deadbolt lock *(left, top)* and a key-in-knob lock *(left, center)*. The deadlatch design of a key-in-knob lock has a small plunger alongside the spring latch, which protects the latch assembly from being pushed back by a plastic card. On a deadbolt lock, turning its key or thumb-turn knob slides a 1-inch bolt from the door into the strike jamb.

The door locks in many older houses are often of the mortise-lock variety *(left, bottom)*. These locks combine a latch and a deadbolt and contain their workings inside a metal case. The lock case fits into a large rectangular cavity cut into the door's edge. Locking buttons near the bottom of the edge plate lock the handle without a key.

Troubleshooting

Problem

Solution

Problem	Solution
• **Key won't fit in keyhole**	Pick foreign matter clear of keyhole with needle or awl; if material won't come out, remove cylinder (deadbolt **74**; rim lock **75**; mortise lock **77**; key-in-knob lock **76**) • Remove broken cylinder for service (deadbolt **74**; rim lock **75**; mortise lock **77**; key-in-knob lock **76**) •
• **Key stuck in lock**	Pull key out slowly with pliers and lubricate keyhole **70** • Disassemble lock and tighten loose cylinder retaining plate screws (deadbolt **74**; rim lock **75**) •
• **Key turns in keyhole but doesn't lock**	Remove broken cylinder for service (deadbolt **74**; rim lock **75**; mortise lock **77**; key-in-knob lock **76**) •
• **Key broken in lock**	Pick broken piece out with needle or awl; if key won't come out, remove cylinder (deadbolt **74**; rim lock **75**; mortise lock **77**; key-in-knob lock **76**) and push out key •
• **Key doesn't turn in keyhole or turns stiffly**	Lubricate keyhole or bolt **70** • Adjust binding strike plate **44** • Remove dirty or gummed-up cylinder for service (deadbolt **74**; rim lock **75**; mortise lock **77**; key-in-knob lock **76**) and lubricate **80** • Remove dirty assembly **78** for cleaning and lubrication **80** • Remove dirty lock case (rim lock **75**; mortise lock **78**) for cleaning and lubrication **80** • Replace broken bolt assembly **78** • Thaw frozen cylinder with an antifreeze spray •
• **Bolt doesn't enter bolt hole**	Realign strike plate **44** •
• **Doorknob of key-in-lock knob turns but bolt doesn't move**	Replace broken bolt assembly **78** • Replace broken tailpiece of the key-in-knob lock **76** •

Before You Start

Most lock repairs, including replacing a cylinder, can be handled by the homeowner.

Repairing a broken door lock may seem like a daunting project. After all, the lock was designed to keep even the most experienced intruder at bay. But in most cases, the lock can be disassembled for cleaning and lubrication, and the homeowner can remove the cylinder and lock case. Replacing a cylinder on a modern lock is easy: just get an exact replacment from a locksmith. The cyclinders in older lock cases, however, are best replaced by a locksmith.

COMMON PROBLEMS

Most lock problems stem either from lack of proper maintenance or from abuse to the lock cylinder. If the lock doesn't work, first inspect your key; it may be burred or bent or it may be the wrong key altogether. Remove burrs with emery cloth and replace bent keys.

Many solutions to common lock problems involve disassembling the lock for cleaning or repairs. Leave the servicing of lock cases to a professional. Although the covers of rim locks and mortise locks are removable, they enclose an intricate assemblage of levers, slides, and springs that are difficult to put back once they've fallen out.

Before You StartTips:

⋯⟩ Have a spare key on hand when working on a lock—just in case you damage the original or break it in the lock.

⋯⟩ Force is not the answer. If a cylinder won't turn, don't force it. Instead, remove and replace it, or have a locksmith refurbish it.

TOOLS

Screwdriver
Electric drill
Drill guide
Spade bits
Channel-joint pliers
Utility knife
File
Chisel
Awl
Hole saw

MATERIALS

Powdered graphite
Spray silicone lubricant
Petroleum-based spray lubricant
Light machine oil
Mineral spirits

SAFETY FIRST

Wear rubber gloves and safety glasses, and follow all manufacturer's instructions when cleaning lock parts with solvents.

Easing a Sticking Lock

LUBRICATING A LOCK

• Lubricate a lock twice a year. Choose one lubricant and stick with it; mixing lubricants can gum up the lock, requiring disassembly and thorough cleaning *(page 80)*.

• One of the best lubricants is graphite powder, puffed from a tube. Press the nozzle into the keyhole and into the cracks around the bolt and squeeze it once or twice *(right)*.

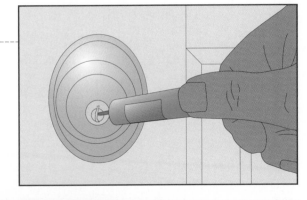

LUBRICATING A LATCH

• Another effective lubricant is petroleum-based lubricant spray. Fix the plastic straw in the nozzle to focus spray into the key-hole and around the bolt *(right)*. Spray liberally to saturate the assembly, then wipe off the excess with a rag. After applying any lubricant, insert the key and work the bolt back and forth to help it penetrate the lock.

REMOVING A BROKEN KEY
Snap. That stubborn old lock finally ate a key. But instead of calling a locksmith, grab a screwdriver and disassemble the lock *(page 74)*. Once you have the cylinder out, insert a bent paper clip into the back end of the cylinder and push the broken key out *(right)*. Before reassembling, take the time to clean and lubricate the lock. Dirt and old lubricants probably caused the lock to stick in the first place.

Installing a Deadbolt Lock

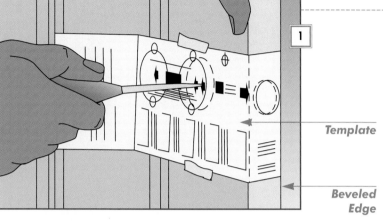

Template

Beveled Edge

1. USING THE TEMPLATE

Most lock manufacturers supply paper templates to indicate the position and size of holes you need to drill. Always read the instructions before you start.

• Fit the template over the high side of the door—that is, its beveled edge *(page 49)*—and tape it in place.

• Then, with an awl, mark where you need to drill on the door face for the cylinder and on the door edge for the bolt *(left)*.

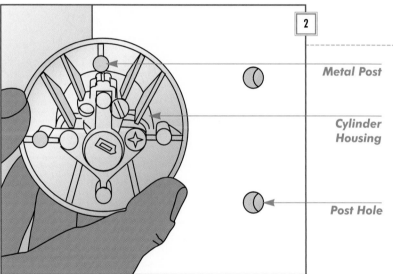

Metal Post

Cylinder Housing

Post Hole

2. DRILLING SMALLER HOLES

Some single-cylinder tubular deadbolts *(left)* have two metal posts protruding from the back of the cylinder. These posts fit in the door and keep the cylinder from being twisted out during a potential break-in.

• Since these holes overlap the larger cylinder hole, it's best to drill them first. These holes then provide a place for sawdust, created when you're drilling the cylinder hole, to escape, which reduces the likelihood of clogging the teeth of the hole saw *(Step 3)*.

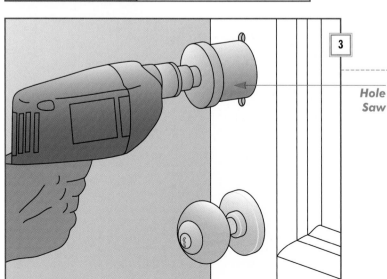

Hole Saw

3. DRILLING A HOLE FOR THE CYLINDER

• Remove the template and wedge the door open with shims.

• Fit a power drill with a hole saw specified by the lock manufacturer, and drill the cylinder hole *(left)*.

CAUTION: *To prevent splintering, stop drilling when the pilot bit of the hole saw pierces through the door. Pull out the saw, and finish the hole from the other side of the door.*

4. Boring the bolt hole

• Fit the drill with a spade bit and a drill guide, and drill a hole perpendicular to the door edge *(right)*.

• Blow out any sawdust and insert the bolt assembly.

• Etch around the outline of the edge plate with a utility knife.

• Remove the assembly, and with a chisel and hammer, chip a mortise so the edge plate fits flush.

• Re-insert the assembly, mark and drill the mounting holes, and screw the edge plate in place.

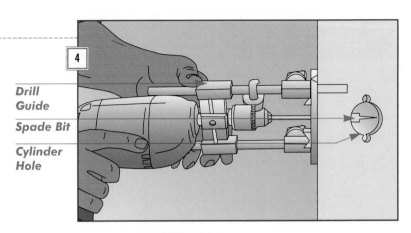

Drill Guide

Spade Bit

Cylinder Hole

5. Installing the cylinder housing

• Before completing installation, check whether the deadbolt retracts and extends as it should by inserting the tip of a screwdriver through the slot in the bolt assembly and working it back and forth.

• If the deadbolt slides freely, install the cylinder housing on the outside of the door. Hold the housing so the notched end of the keyhole points up, and push the tailpiece through the slot *(right)*.

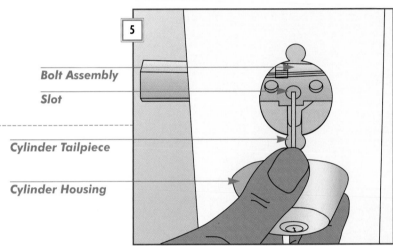

Bolt Assembly

Slot

Cylinder Tailpiece

Cylinder Housing

6. Attaching the retaining plate

• Position the retaining plate against the cylinder hole on the inside of the door, and screw it through the door into the back of the cylinder housing *(right)*.

Cylinder Retaining Plate

7. Installing the thumb-turn assembly

• Now you can screw the thumb-turn over the retaining plate *(right)*.

• When you have finished, check that the lock works with the door open before installing the strike plate *(page 73)*.

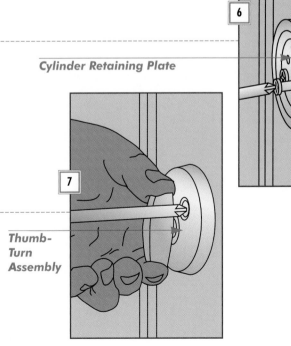

Thumb-Turn Assembly

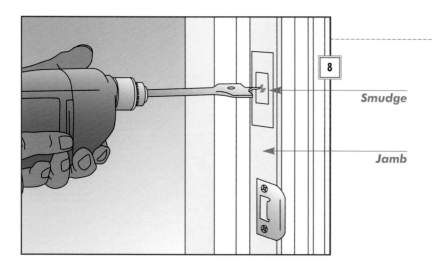

Smudge

Jamb

8. BORING THE STRIKE HOLE

• First, rub a crayon on the end of the dead-bolt. Retract the bolt, close the door, and turn the key to force the deadbolt against the door jamb.

• The smudge on the jamb indicates the location of the strike hole. Position the strike plate with the mark centered in the opening and outline the plate and plate opening.

• Then with a spade bit, bore a hole in the jamb slightly larger than the deadbolt *(left)*.

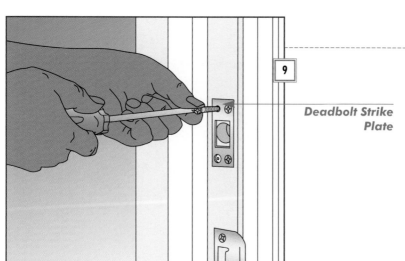

Deadbolt Strike Plate

9. SECURING THE STRIKE PLATE

• Cut a mortise with a wood chisel and a hammer so the plate will fit flush with the jamb.

• Mark the screw positions in the mortise, drill pilot holes, and screw the strike plate in place *(left)*. Many manufacturers provide 3-inch screws to attach the strike plate so you can reach the stud behind the jamb. If your screws are short, replace them with longer ones for added security.

Ron's TRADE SECRETS

ACCURATELY MARKING SCREW HOLES

Sometimes no matter how careful you are in marking the screw hole locations for a piece of door hardware (like a strike plate or edge plate), the holes you drill end up misaligned.

An easy way to prevent this is to hold the hardware in place, insert a Phillips-head screwdriver into each screw hole, and push it into the wood or give it a tap with a hammer. Doing so leaves a set of crosshairs embedded in the wood to indicate the exact center. You can also use a self-centering bit designed just for this purpose.

Replacing a Deadbolt Cylinder

1. REMOVING THE RETAINING SCREWS

- To remove the cylinder housing from a deadbolt lock for cleaning or servicing, unscrew the thumb-turn and remove the two screws securing the cylinder retaining plate to the door.

- Lift off the retaining plate and the cylinder housing.

- Remove the cylinder retaining screws from the back of the housing *(right)*.

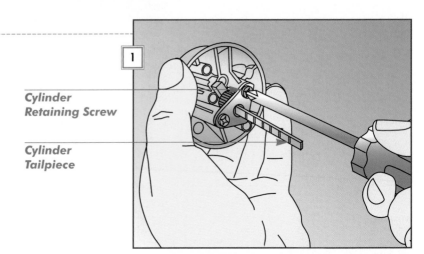

Cylinder Retaining Screw

Cylinder Tailpiece

2. REMOVING THE CYLINDER

- Pull out the cylinder by its tailpiece *(right)*. Take it to a locksmith for repair or to buy an exact replacment.

- To reassemble, slide the cylinder back into the housing and secure it with the retaining screws. Add the retaining plate and install the mounting screws. Attach the thumb-turn with its screws.

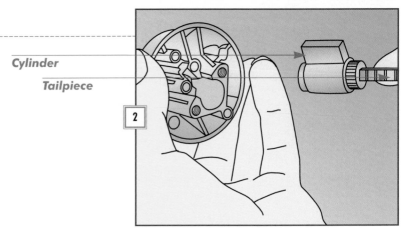

Cylinder

Tailpiece

Replacing a Rim Lock Cylinder

1. REMOVING THE RETAINING SCREWS

Rim locks may have vertical deadbolts *(right)* or horizontal ones.

- To give the lock case of either type a thorough cleaning *(page 80)* or to take out the cylinder for servicing, remove the screws that secure the lock to the door *(right)*.

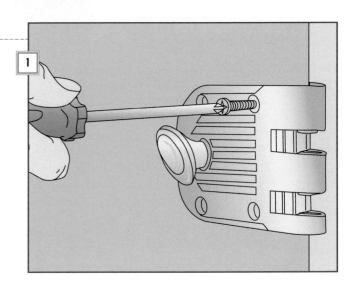

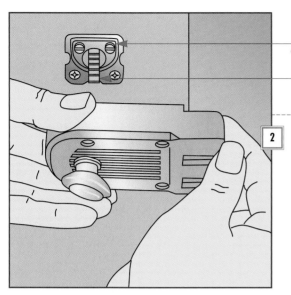

Cylinder Retaining
Plate

Cylinder Tailpiece

2. REMOVING THE LOCK CASE

● Pull the lock case gently off to expose the cylinder retaining plate with its tailpiece protruding through the center *(left)*.

CAUTION: *Do not risk damaging the inner workings of the lock by opening the lock case.*

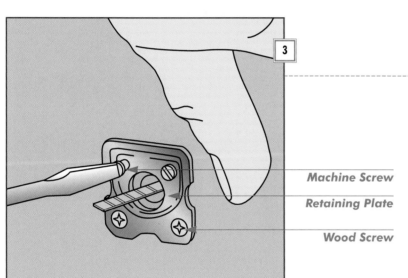

Machine Screw

Retaining Plate

Wood Screw

3. REMOVING THE RETAINING PLATE

● To free the cylinder, remove the two machine screws that pass through the retaining plate and door into the cylinder on the other side *(left)*.

● In some locks, the retaining plate is fastened to the door with two wood screws. Remove these screws with a screwdriver to free the retaining plate.

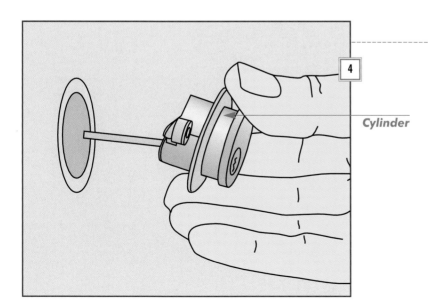

Cylinder

4. EXTRACTING THE CYLINDER

● As you take out the last screw, support the cylinder with one hand to prevent it from falling out *(left)*.

● Clean the cylinder *(page 80)*, re-install it, or take it to a locksmith for a replacement.

● To re-install the lock, attach the cylinder retaining plate and insert the cylinder through the door with the keyhole's notched edge up. Fit the lock case over the tailpiece and screw the case in place.

Replacing a Key-in-Knob Lock Cylinder

1. REMOVING THE KNOBS

The cylinder housing of a key-in-knob lock is the exterior knob. You must remove both doorknobs to free the cylinder.

• Unfasten the screws on the inside escutcheon plate *(right)*.

• With these screws removed, pull the inside and outside knobs apart. On some models you must remove the inside knob; depress a release catch on the knob's neck *(page 43)* and then pull the knob off its shaft to reveal the screw.

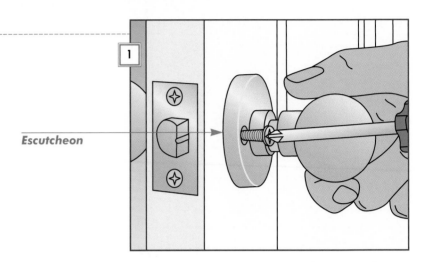

Escutcheon

2. REMOVING THE CYLINDER

• Insert the key, then pull on the tailpiece while you turn the key 45 degrees counterclockwise. Withdraw the key; the cylinder and knob face will separate from the knob shell *(right)*.

• To re-install the cylinder, insert the key in the cylinder. Turn the key and cylinder 45 degrees counterclockwise, fit the cylinder between the prongs of the bracket inside the knob's shell, and press it in place. Turn the key clockwise until you hear a snap.

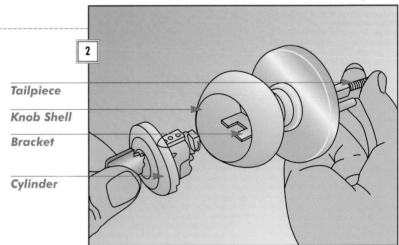

Tailpiece

Knob Shell

Bracket

Cylinder

Removing a Mortise Lock Cylinder

1. TAKING OFF THE FACEPLATE

• Before removing a cylinder for repair or replacement, check whether the lock case edge plate is hidden by a faceplate. If so, remove its screws and lift the faceplate off *(right)*.

• Loosen the top and bottom lock case screws about two complete turns.

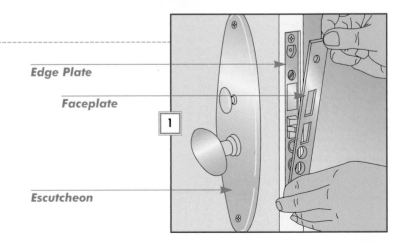

Edge Plate

Faceplate

Escutcheon

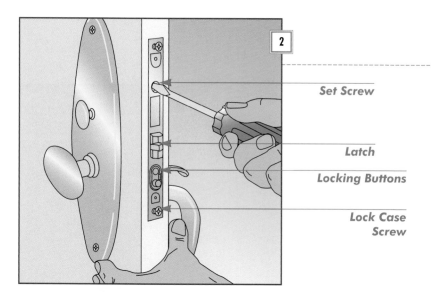

Set Screw

Latch

Locking Buttons

Lock Case
Screw

2. FREEING THE CYLINDER

• The cylinder is held in the door by a set screw. Loosen it three or four turns with a screwdriver *(left)*.

• Some models have a second set screw on the inside edge of the lock case that connects to the thumb-turn; do not loosen this screw.

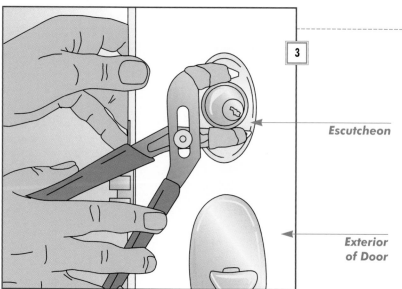

Escutcheon

Exterior
of Door

3. UNSCREWING THE CYLINDER

• To protect the cylinder's finish, gently grip the rim of the cylinder with channel-joint pliers padded with masking tape and turn it counterclockwise to loosen it *(left)*. Count the number of rotations to ensure proper assembly later.

• Some cylinders have rotating collars that prevent them from being loosened in this way. For such a cylinder, instead insert the key partway and use it to gently turn the cylinder.

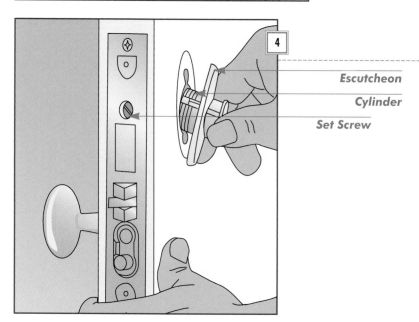

Escutcheon

Cylinder

Set Screw

4. REMOVING THE CYLINDER

• Remove the cylinder by unscrewing it the rest of the way by hand *(left),* again counting the number of rotations.

• To re-install the cylinder, insert it in the door with the keyhole's notched edge pointing up. Taking care to keep the threads of the cylinder in line with those of the lock case, rotate it by hand the same number of times as for removal.

• Then retighten the set screw and top and bottom lock case screws.

Replacing a Bolt or Deadlatch

1. UNSCREWING THE EDGE PLATE

- To disassemble a key-in-knob deadlatch, first remove the doorknobs *(page 76)*. If you are working on a deadbolt assembly, take off the thumb-turn, cylinder retaining plate, and cylinder housing *(page 72)*.

- Unscrew the edge plate *(right)*.

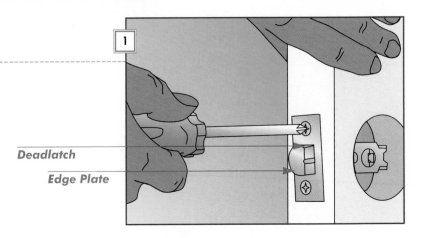

Deadlatch

Edge Plate

2. REMOVING THE BOLT ASSEMBLY

- Pull the deadlatch free *(right)*. Some bolt assemblies in metal doors have no retaining screws. Push this type of deadbolt out of the door by inserting a screwdriver through the knob opening and behind the latch.

- To reassemble, insert the bolt or latch in the mortise in the door's edge and secure it with screws. For key-in-knob locks, slide the knob tailpiece through the slot in the latch assembly, add the remaining knob, and secure it with screws. On a deadlatch, add the cylinder, fasten the retaining plate with screws, and re-install the thumb-turn.

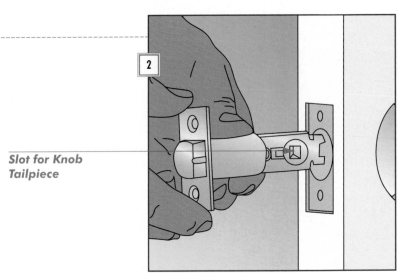

Slot for Knob
Tailpiece

Removing a Mortised Lock Case

1. FREEING THE ESCUTCHEON

- To extract a lock for cleaning or repair, first take its cylinder out of the lock case *(page 76)*. Then loosen the set screw for the inside knob and remove the knob.

- Unscrew the screws at the top and bottom of the escutcheon on the inside of the door, and lift it off *(right)*. The thumb-turn and its shaft are attached to the escutcheon and come away with it.

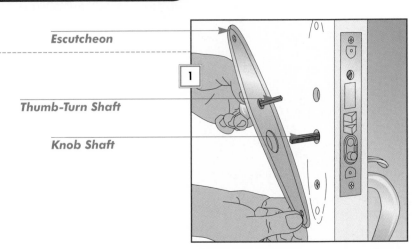

Escutcheon

Thumb-Turn Shaft

Knob Shaft

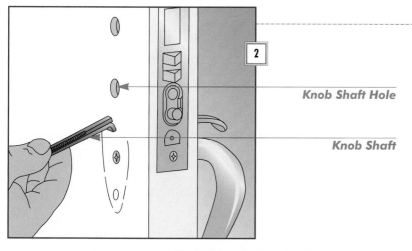

Knob Shaft Hole

Knob Shaft

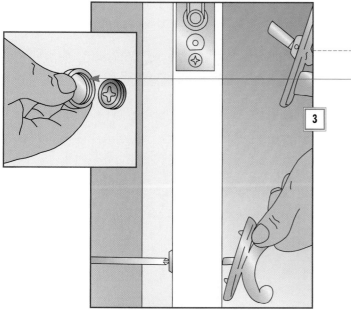

Screw Cover

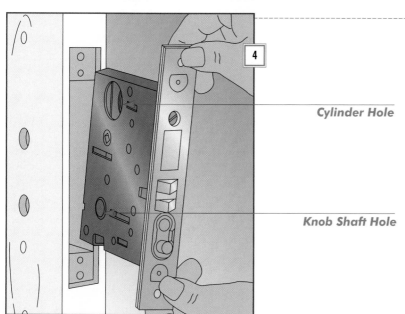

Cylinder Hole

Knob Shaft Hole

2. EXTRACTING THE KNOB SHAFT

• If your lock has knobs on both the exterior and interior, the shaft will be a simple square one. Pull it free from the door and skip to Step 4.

• For a lock with a handle on the outside *(left)*, the knob shaft likely consists of a straight and a hooked piece; together they form a square shaft.

• Pry the ends apart and slide the straight piece out. Then unhook the bottom piece and pull it free.

3. DETACHING THE EXTERIOR HANDLE

• Unscrew the screw on the inside of the door that secures the top of the handle.

• A decorative cover often hides the head of the bottom screw. Using channel-joint pliers padded with masking tape, loosen the cover, then take it off by hand *(inset)*.

• Finish removing the bottom screw while you support the handle on the outside *(left)*.

4. FREEING THE LOCK CASE

• If there's paint buildup, use a utility knife to score around the edge plate.

• Then with a screwdriver, remove the screws at the top and bottom of the edge plate, and lift out the entire lock case *(left)*.

• Clean the lock case thoroughly *(page 80)*, or take it to a locksmith for service.

• To reassemble a mortise lock, slide the lock case into the mortise and secure it with the lock case screws. Reattach the handle and insert the knob shaft pieces through the knob shaft hole. Screw the escutcheon in place, slip the doorknob over the shaft, and tighten its set scew. Finally, replace the cylinder *(page 76)*.

Cleaning and Lubricating a Lock Case

1. WASHING THE LOCK CASE

● Working in a well-ventilated area, and wearing rubber gloves, wash dirty lock parts such as bolt assemblies, cylinders, and lock cases in a shallow basin of mineral spirits or turpentine *(right)*.

● Clean the bolt assemblies of key-in-knob and deadbolt locks with a cotton swab.

 CAUTION: *Do not open the lock case; instead brush solvent into the openings.*

2. DRYING THE LOCK CASE

● Set clean lock parts on a newspaper to drain for an hour or so. You can hasten drying of a lock case with a hair dryer set at low heat *(right)*.

 CAUTION: *Dispose safely of all dirty solvents, cleaning rags, and papers in accordance with your local regulations. Cap solvent containers and store them in a nonflammable storage locker.*

3. LUBRICATING THE LOCK CASE

● Generously apply light machine oil through the holes scattered over the surface of the case cover plates *(right)*.

● Also, oil the surface of a deadlatch or deadbolt assembly and lubricate the cylinder. In dry, dusty environments, use powdered graphite.

Replacing a Patio Door Cylinder

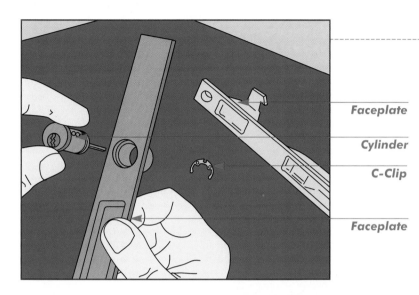

Faceplate

Cylinder

C-Clip

Faceplate

REPLACING THE CYLINDER

• To remove the lock on a sliding patio door for repair or replacement, take out the two screws on the inside faceplate that pass through the door and thread into the exterior faceplate.

• Once the screws are out, pull the two halves apart.

• On some patio door locks, you can re-place the cylinder by removing the C-clip on the end of the barrel that houses the cylinder *(left)*.

Maintaining a Storm Door Latch

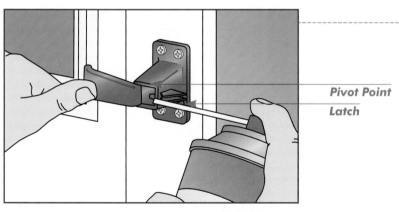

Pivot Point

Latch

LUBRICATING THE DOOR LATCH

With constant use and exposure to the ele-ments, the latches on most storm doors eventually become balky.

• Push on the inside handle to expose its pivot point, and spray this area with lubri-cant *(left)*.

• Next, spray the latch with lubricant and wipe off any excess. In dusty climates, use powdered graphite.

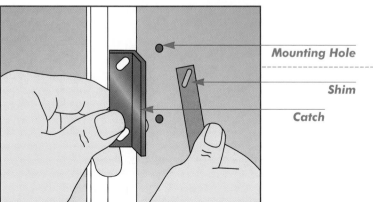

Mounting Hole

Shim

Catch

ADJUSTING THE DOOR CATCH

Over time, the door catch that attaches to the jamb can wear and fail to engage the latch properly.

• If this happens, raise the catch with a shim made from cardboard *(left)* so that the latch engages the catch.

FIX IT: Panes & Screens

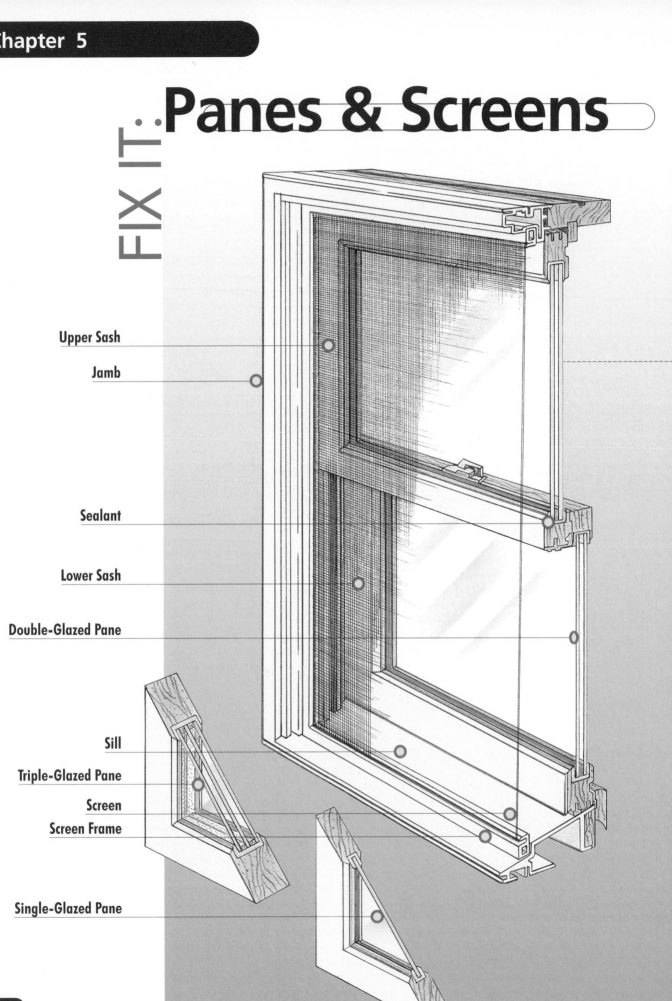

Upper Sash

Jamb

Sealant

Lower Sash

Double-Glazed Pane

Sill

Triple-Glazed Pane

Screen

Screen Frame

Single-Glazed Pane

Chapter 5

How They Work

A double-glazed or insulating window *(top left)* has two parallel sheets of glass separated by metal bars around their edges. An elastic sealant applied to the perimeter of the pane holds the glass and bars in place and prevents air from entering or leaving the space between the sheets of glass. This dead-air space works as an insulator.

A double-glazed window insulates two to three times better than a typical single thickness of glass *(lower left)* but costs four times as much. A triple-glazed window *(center left),* which features two dead-air spaces, insulates two to three times better than the double-glazed variety but costs roughly twice as much. Consequently they are economical only in the coldest climates.

To admit fresh air while excluding pests, most windows and special exterior doors accept screens. The mesh may be made of either fiberglass or aluminum. In both cases a rubber strip, called a spline, locks the screening into a channel in the frame.

Contents

Troubleshooting

Problem	**Solution**
• **Single-pane window cracked or broken**	Cut new glass **86**, and reglaze window **88** •
• **Window offers poor insulating properties**	Replace single-pane with insulating window **90** •
• **Curved glass in window broken or cracked**	Cut new glass **87**, and reglaze window **88** •
• **Glass pane rattles**	Replace deteriorating glazing compound **88** •
• **Double- or triple-pane window cracked or broken**	Reglaze the window **90** •
• **Double- or triple-pane window foggy**	Reglaze the window **90** •
• **Acrylic pane cracked or yellow**	Cut new pane of glass or acrylic **86,** and reglaze window **88** •
• **Screen torn**	Patch screen **93** • Replace screen **94** •

Before You Start

Developments in windows—such as double glazing and plastic panes—require that you know more about your windows before attempting repairs.

NEW GLASS

You can identify a multi-glazed window by placing your fingers on opposite sides of the glass. If your fingers appear to touch, it's a single pane; a gap of 1/2 inch indicates a double pane; 3/4 inch or greater is likely a triple pane. For a single-glazed window, you can cut replacement panes yourself (*page 86*); even curved panes are simple to cut (*page 87*). However, you must order replacement panes for double- or triple-glazed windows from a window specialist.

NEW SCREENS

The screens that fit over most windows and doors are simple to repair or replace. Fiberglass screening (*page 94*) is the easiest to install but tends to sag. Aluminum screening (*page 95*) is more expensive but stronger—though it eventually oxidizes in humid climates.

Before You Start Tips:

···⟩ Panes of shatter-resistant glass or plastic must be used in certain applications, such as doors. Check with a glazier.

···⟩ Cutting glass or rescreening a door calls for a large, flat work surface. A hollow-core door laid across sawhorses is just the ticket. You can often find a scratched or nicked door at a lumberyard for just a few dollars.

TOOLS

Carpenter's square
Glass cutter
Glass pliers
Chisel
Long-nose pliers
Caulking gun
Paintbrush
Putty knife
Utility knife
Hammer
Splining tool
C-clamps

MATERIALS

Caulk
Glazing compound
Glazier's points
Linseed oil
Sandpaper
Neoprene blocks
Metal or fiberglass screen
Spline

SAFETY FIRST

Wear leather gloves and goggles when working with glass. Carefully sweep or vacuum up glass fragments. Always get help from a friend when lifting multi-pane windows, which can be surprisingly heavy.

Rectangular Window Panes

1. SCORING A STRAIGHT LINE

Except for the tool, there's no difference between cutting glass and acrylic plastic.

• Lay the pane on newspaper and mark the cut line with a permananent marker. A properly cut pane should be approximately 1/4 inch smaller than the opening.

• Wearing gloves, align a straightedge with the mark and dip the wheel of a glass cutter in kerosene. Starting at the far edge of the glass, pull the cutter toward you in one steady stroke *(right)*. Apply even pressure until you reach the end of the cut. Score an acrylic pane with an acrylic cutter *(inset)*.

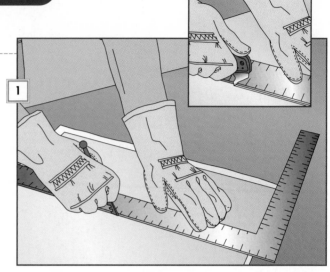

2. COMPLETING THE CUT

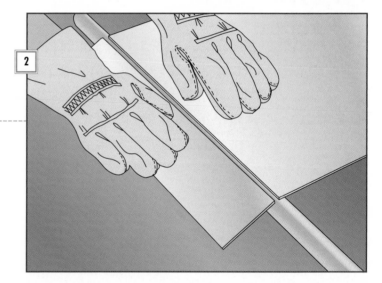

• For glass, place a dowel or broom handle directly under the score line. When cutting acrylic, position the score line at the edge of a work table.

• Press down firmly on both sides of the material to snap it *(right)*.

Ron's TRADE SECRETS

WORKING AT THE EDGE
When I cut a pane for a window, I often need to trim a narrow strip from a piece of glass. To get a clean break, I cut a 1/2-inch-deep groove (or kerf) in the edge a piece of wood at least as long as the edge of the pane. While a table saw works best, a handsaw will do. Or, you can glue up strips of 1/8-inch hardboard or plywood to form a U. Then after scoring a line with a glass cutter, simply slip your new tool onto the edge of the glass and push down on the tool to snap the glass *(right)*.

Curved Window Panes

Pattern

1. SCORING A CURVED LINE

- Trace the shape of a curved pane onto a piece of cardboard and trim it with scissors to make a pattern.

- With the pattern as a guide, score the glass as described on page 86, drawing the glass cutter close and steady around the edge of the pattern *(left)*.

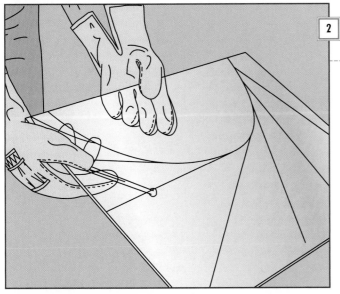

2. DEEPENING THE SCORE LINES

- Score several straight lines radiating from the curve to the edge of the glass.

- Then deepen each curve by lifting the glass and tapping lightly along the line from underneath with the ball end of the glass cutter *(left)*.

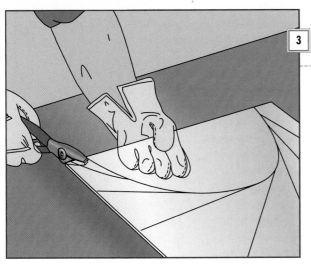

3. SNAPPING THE CURVE

- Snap off the scored segments with glass pliers *(left)*.

- If any jagged edges remain along the curve, nip away about 1/16 inch at a time with glass pliers until the edge is uniform.

- Smooth any roughness with fine sandpaper.

Chapter 5

Repairing a Broken Window

1. REMOVING THE GLASS FRAGMENTS

• Wearing heavy work gloves and safety goggles, start at the top of the window to remove shards of glass. Pull each shard straight out of the sash *(right)*; gently wiggle stubborn fragments free.

 CAUTION: *Remove glass from muntins—strips that divide the panes of a window—with care. Muntins are delicate, and their replacement requires a carpenter's skills.*

2. REMOVING OLD GLAZING COMPOUND

• If the compound has hardened, coat it with linseed oil and let it soak into the compound for 30 minutes. If the compound is painted, soften it with a soldering iron fitted with a 1/4- to 1/2-inch tip.

• Pry old glazing compound out with an old chisel *(right)*.

• Pull the glazier's points from the window frame with long-nose pliers *(inset)* and clean the channel with a wire brush.

 CAUTION: *When using a soldering iron, be careful not to burn adjacent wood.*

Glazing Compound

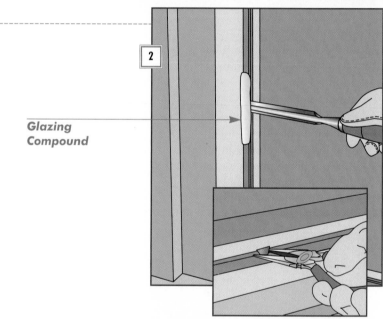

3. PREPARING THE "BED"

There are two common glazing compounds used to form a "bed" for the glass: an elastic type, dispensed from a tube, and glazing putty that comes in a tin.

• Depending on the compound you chose, you may first need to prime the channel; follow the manufacturer's instructions.

• To apply the elastic type, squeeze a uniform 3/8-inch bead in the channel *(right)*.

• For glazing putty, roll it into a snakelike shape *(inset)*, then press it into the channel.

Putty-Type Glazing Compound

Elastic-Type Glazing Compound

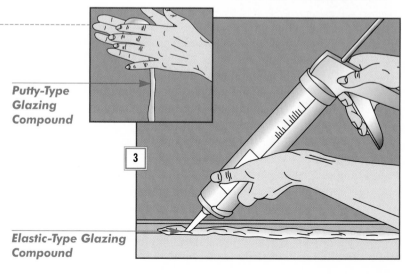

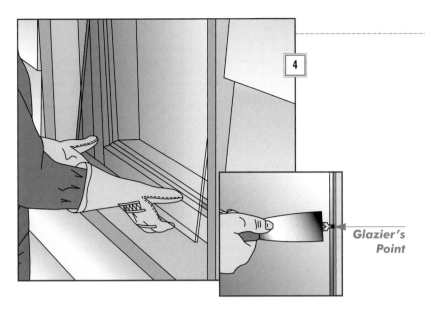

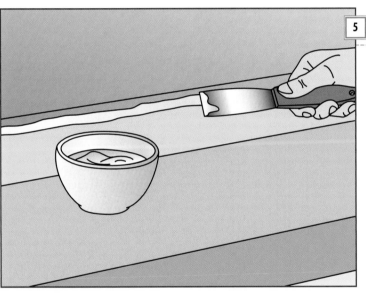

Glazier's Point

4. INSTALLING THE GLASS

• Set the pane into the bed of glazing compound, centering the pane in the opening *(left)*.

• With a stiff putty knife, press glazier's points halfway into the sash and flush against the glass *(inset)*. Position a glazier's point every 6 inches or so, but use at least two points on each side of the pane.

5. COVERING THE GLAZIER'S POINTS

• Apply glazing compound to the joint between the pane and frame as in Step 3.

• For a neat appearance, dip a putty knife in water or light machine oil and draw it over the bead to create a bevel at approximately 45 degrees *(left)*.

• Seal the corners well and trim off excess compound inside and out.

• When the compound is dry—it no longer shows a thumbprint—paint or varnish it.

Ron's TRADE SECRETS

BEVELED PUTTY KNIFE
Creating a perfect bevel on glazing compound is second nature for a professional glazier. Here's a simple way to get the same result without years of experience. To bevel glazing compound with this tool, place the end of the putty knife against the glass *(right)*, and draw the bevel across the glazing compound.

Replacing an Insulating Pane

ANATOMY

An insulating window sits in a rabbet cut into the edge of the frame. Wood molding *(near right)* or a snap-on glazing bead *(far right)* holds it in place. The window or door manufacturer may or may not insert neoprene blocks between the pane and the frame to both center and cushion the pane. Reuse original blocks whenever possible. If you need to replace them, order a new set from a window repair specialist.

CAUTION: *To keep glass from rubbing against metal and eventually breaking, always use neoprene blocks when replacing an insulating window in a metal frame.*

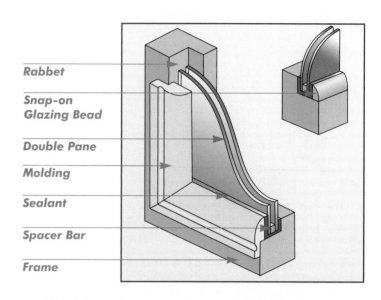

Rabbet

Snap-on
Glazing Bead

Double Pane

Molding

Sealant

Spacer Bar

Frame

1. CUTTING THE SEALANT

• Before removing the molding, measure between the moldings and add 1 inch to each measurement to determine the size of the replacement unit.

• Slip a utility knife between the molding and the window to cut any sealant you find *(right).* Then unscrew the molding or pry it free with a stiff putty knife.

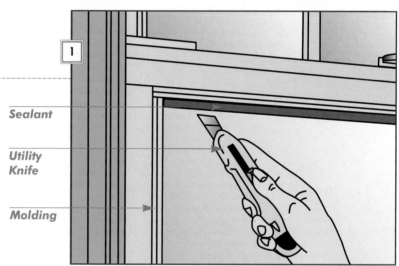

1

Sealant

Utility
Knife

Molding

2. REPLACING THE WINDOW

• If the window is in one piece, lift it out of the frame *(right);* wear gloves, and get help if it's heavy. Otherwise, remove the broken pieces and edges from the sash *(page 88).*

• Scrape old sealant from the sash and molding. Remove neoprene blocks, if any.

• Place the new window in the sash (using the old neoprene blocks); and if it had any sealant, apply a new bead.

• Resecure the molding using wood screws every 8 to 10 inches, or snap it in place.

2

New Insulating Glass for a Door

1. PREPARING THE DOOR

Only wood doors with solid stiles and rails at least 1-3/4 inches thick are suitable for a double-pane insulating window.

● Check the door frame for square *(left)*. If it isn't, you may be able to square it by tightening loose joints *(page 54)*. Otherwise, shim the pane with neoprene blocks *(Step 3)*.

● Measure the height and width of the opening and add 1 inch to each. Order a double-pane window of these dimensions.

● After the replacement window has arrived, remove the molding and sealant and, wearing work gloves, lift out the old pane.

1-by-2 Guide

Rabbet

2. ENLARGING THE RABBET

● To determine the width of the rabbet, add 1/2 inch to the width of the new window, and subtract the width of the opening. Divide the result in half to identify the rabbet bit size. Calculate the top and bottom rabbets the same way.

● For rabbet depth, add 3/4 inch to the thickness of the double pane.

● Tack a board beside the window opening as a router guide, then cut the rabbets in a series of 3/8-inch-deep passes *(left)*.

● Square the corners with a chisel.

3. PREPARING THE RABBET

● Drill 1/4-inch drainage holes at 6-inch intervals at the back of the rabbet with a power drill *(left)*. Angle the holes downward toward the outside. Blow sawdust out of the rabbet.

● To cushion the pane in the frame, lay neoprene blocks at equal intervals along the bottom rabbet.

● If the pane doesn't sit square to the sides of the frame, add blocks to shim it square.

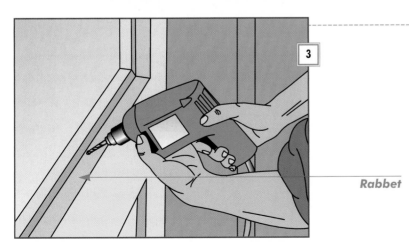

Rabbet

4. SEALING THE WINDOW

- Apply a 1/4-inch bead of elastic-type sealant with a caulking gun along the back edge of the rabbet *(right)*.

- With a helper, rest the bottom edge of the window on the neoprene blocks.

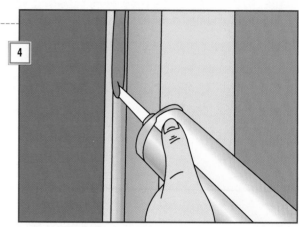

5. ADDING NEOPRENE BLOCKS

- Slip neoprene blocks around the perimeter of the window about every 8 to 10 inches to center the window in the frame *(right)*.

- Then press the edges of the pane gently into the sealant.

- Fill the voids between the blocks with sealant.

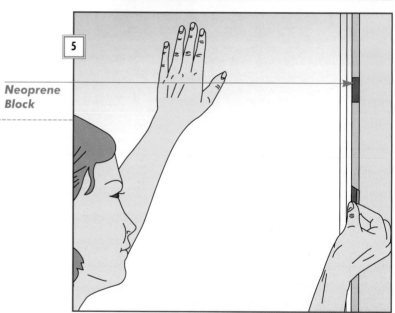

Neoprene
Block

6. ADDING THE MOLDING

- Apply a bead of sealant to the joint between the window edge and the rabbet around the perimeter *(page 89)*.

- Temporarily tack the molding in place with finishing nails *(right)*, then screw it to the door frame every 8 inches.

 CAUTION: *Be sure neither molding nails nor screws contact the glass.*

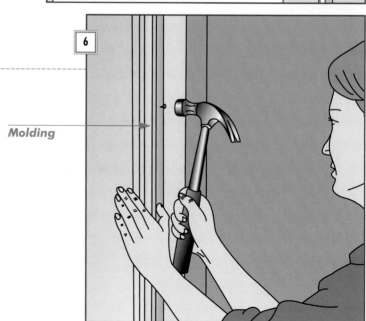

Molding

Patching Screens

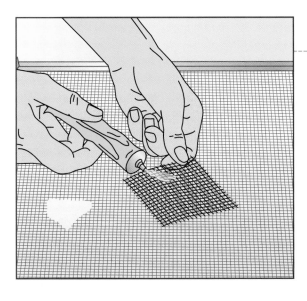

FIBERGLASS

• Repair tiny holes in a fiberglass screen by applying a few drops of cyanoacrylate, or "instant," glue.

• To repair a larger hole *(left)*, make a patch from leftover screening that is large enough to cover the hole.

• Coat the edges of the patch and the area around the hole with a thin coat of glue, then press the patch over the hole.

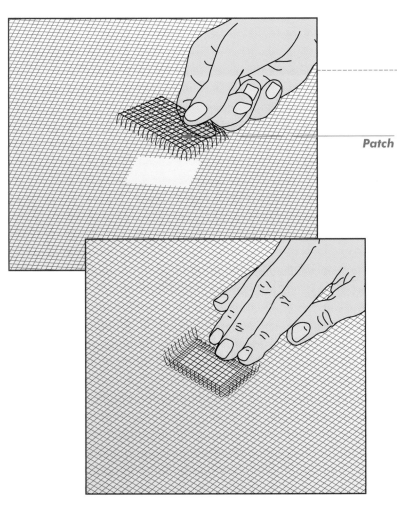

Patch

METAL

• Seal tiny holes in an aluminum screen with a few drops of waterproof glue, such as epoxy.

• To repair a larger hole, first cut the hole square with scissors. Then cut a patch of matching screening about 2 inches wider and longer than the hole.

• Pull several strands of wire out of each edge and bend the remaining wires down over the sides *(left, top)*.

• Position the patch evenly over the hole and work the wires through the screening.

• Turn the screen over, pull the patch tight, and bend the wires down against the screen *(left, bottom)*.

New Screening for a Wood Door

1. REMOVING MOLDING AND SCREENING

• Unscrew the hinges, remove the door, and lay it on a work table. Place a block of wood under each end of the door and attach C-clamps to the frame at its midpoint to bow the frame.

• Lift the molding around the screening with a utility bar *(right)*.

• With a screwdriver, pry loose the staples that hold the screening to the door. Wearing gloves if working with metal screening, pull the screening off the frame.

2. STAPLING SCREENING TO THE FRAME

• Cut new screening 4 inches wider and longer than the opening in the door. Lay the screening on the door, aligning the weave with the frame.

• Staple the screening every 3 inches at a right angle to the frame at one end *(right)*. Do the same at the other end.

• Release the clamps to pull the screen taut, and staple both sides *(inset)*.

• Trim excess screening and replace the molding.

Fastening Screening to a Metal Frame

1. REMOVING THE SPLINE

• With the door or window on a flat surface, dig up one corner of the spline with a screwdriver *(inset)* and pull the spline out of its channel *(right)*.

• Wearing work gloves, pull the old screening from the channel and discard it.

• Lay the new screening over the frame and trim it so it extends 1 inch beyond the channel.

Spline

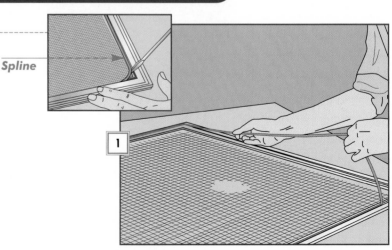

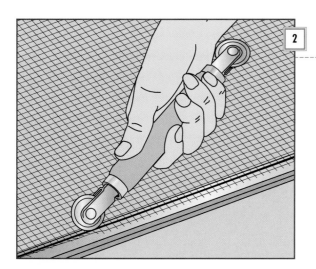

2. CREASING METAL SCREENING

- If re-screening with fiberglass, skip to Step 3.

- To push the edges of aluminum screening into the channel, roll the convex wheel of a splining tool back and forth along the screen at the channel *(left)*.

- Repeat on all sides.

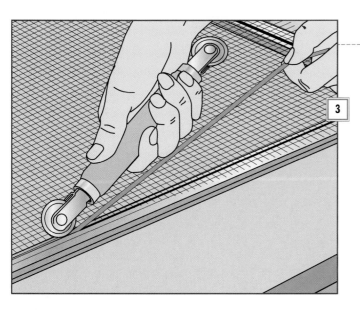

3. INSTALLING THE SPLINE

For long and narrow frames, cut a new spline and install the two short sides first. If the frame is nearly square, install the spline as one piece. The action of the spline pushing the screen into the channel tightens the screen.

- With aluminum screening, force the spline into the channel over the crease you made in Step 2. Use the concave wheel of the splining tool *(left)*. If you're installing fiberglass screening, force the screening and spline together into the channel.

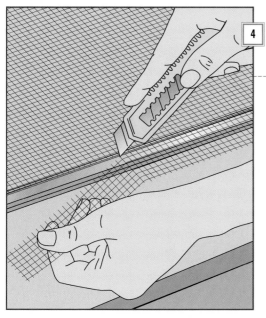

4. TRIMMING THE SCREENING

- Cut off the excess spline. Tuck the ends completely into the channel.

- Then trim the screening close to the spline with a utility knife *(left)*.

FIX IT: Garage Doors

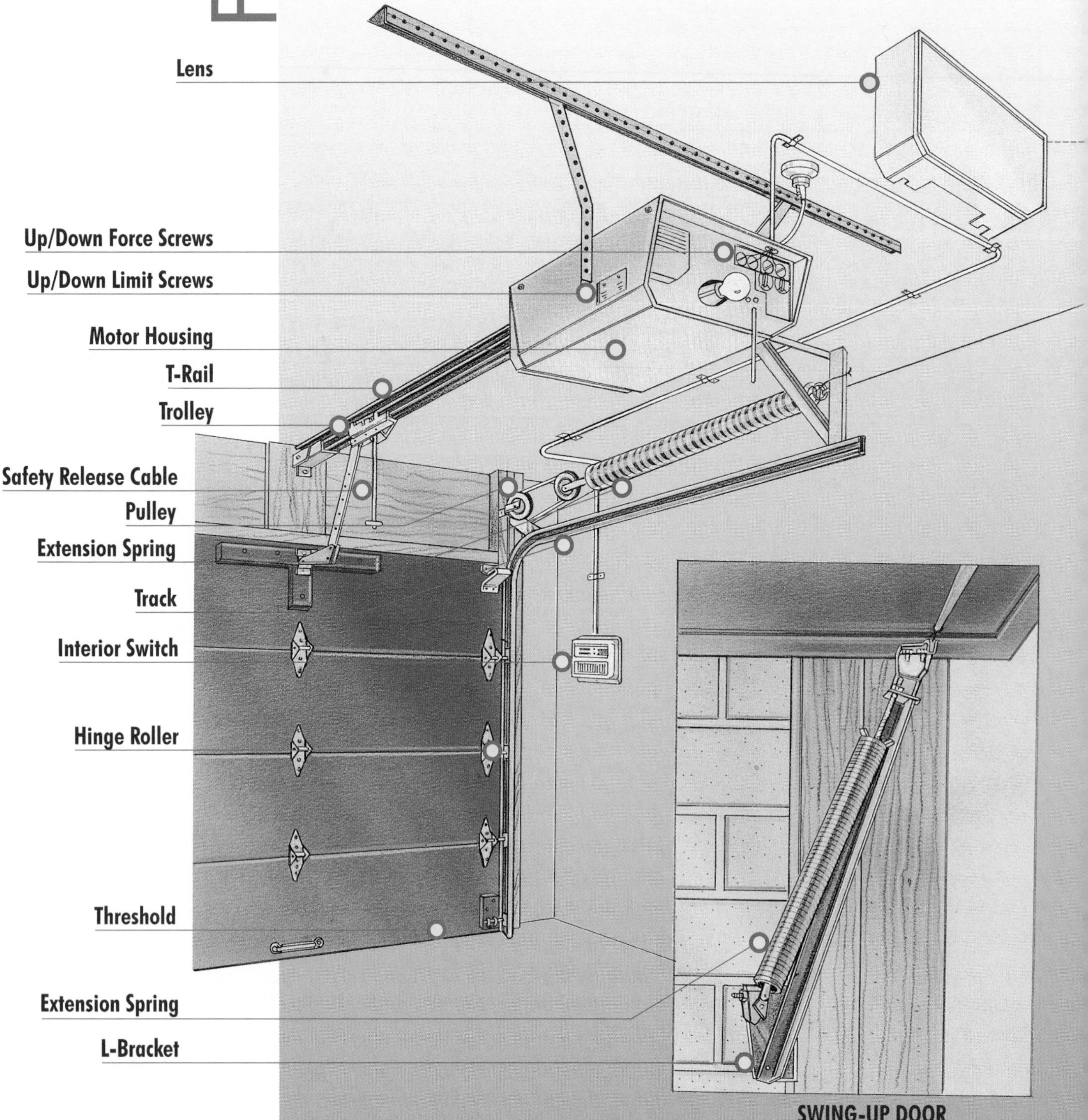

Lens

Up/Down Force Screws

Up/Down Limit Screws

Motor Housing

T-Rail

Trolley

Safety Release Cable

Pulley

Extension Spring

Track

Interior Switch

Hinge Roller

Threshold

Extension Spring

L-Bracket

SWING-UP DOOR

Chapter 6

Contents

How They Work

The sectional garage door at left is shown equipped with an electric garage-door opener. A motor inside the unit turns a screw to raise and lower the door by means of a trolley that rides on a track. Behind a cover on the motor unit is a light bulb, as well as controls for adjusting the mechanism to turn off the motor when the door is fully open or closed and to assure that the motor stops or reverses if a closing door encounters an obstacle.

Springs counterbalance the door for ease of opening and closing. Extension springs, like those shown here, are found at the sides of both multi-panel doors, which roll along overhead tracks, and one-piece doors, which swing out and upward.

Some multi-panel doors have a spring directly above the door. These springs, called torsion springs, are always under considerable tension. Furthermore, repairs and adjustments require special tools. Except for periodic lubrication, torsion springs are best left to a professional.

Troubleshooting

Problem	Solution
• **Water enters garage under door**	Replace worn-out or uneven threshold **107** •
• **Garage door difficult to open**	Clean dirty tracks and lubricate **100** • Replace worn roller **102** • Replace broken spring **105** • Replace broken pulley **104** • Replace broken cable **103** •
• **Garage door opens or closes too easily**	Adjust spring tension to balance door **105** •
• **Automatic opener doesn't open or close door**	Replace dead batteries • Remove obstruction blocking antenna reception • Check to make sure transmitter and receiver codes match • Replace defective transmitter •
• **Automatic opener does not stop when door contacts an object**	Adjust down-force sensitivity **101** •
• **Automatic opener reverses direction or stops before closing door**	Remove object interfering with travel cycle • Adjust down-force sensitivity **101** •
• **Opener reverses direction after closing fully**	Adjust down-limit screw that's improperly set **101** •
• **Automatic opener doesn't open door fully**	Adjust up-limit screw that's improperly set **101** • Adjust up-force screw that's improperly set **101** •
• **Opener motor hums when door reaches fully open or fully closed position**	Adjust up-limit or down-limit screw that's improperly set **101** •
• **Chain rattles when opener is activated**	Increase tension on loose chain **102** •

Before You Start

When a garage door stops partway down or up, the first thing to do is determine whether the problem lies in the door or in the door opener—if you have one.

To find the culprit, pull the safety release cable to disengage the opener from the door *(page 96)*, *then* open and close the door manually. If it works without a hitch, the opener is at fault; if not, the door needs attention.

Start with the Simple Things

More often than not, all a garage door needs to set it right is a good cleaning and oiling of its moving parts. However, other things can go wrong. Pulleys and rollers can wear to the point that lubricating them does no good; you must replace them then. Cables can become slack, and springs can sag more on one side than on the other. Sometimes an adjustment solves the problem; but from time to time, parts need replacing.

Garage-door openers also suffer from neglect. Dirt and hardened grease can gum up the works, immobilizing the drive mechanism. A thorough cleaning could be the remedy. You can solve other problems, such as a door that won't open or close fully—or one that doesn't stop or reverse as it should when it closes on an object in the doorway—with a few simple adjustments of controls inside the motor unit.

Before You StartTips:

⋯⋗ Be careful when working on garage-door springs. Any movement of the door can cause the spring to expand or contract, providing multiple pinch points.

TOOLS

Screwdriver
Adjustable wrench
Paintbrush
Nut driver
C-clamps
Small wire brush
Hammer
Pry bar

MATERIALS

Grease solvent
Cleaning rags
Light machine oil
Galvanized nails
Spray silicone lubricant
Petroleum-based spray lubricant
Powdered graphite

SAFETY FIRST

Whenever you work on a garage door with an automatic opener, unplug the opener before cleaning or adjusting the drive screw or the chain, tracks, or rollers. Secure an open door with C-clamps to prevent the door from accidentally closing.

Maintaining a Garage Door

1. CLEANING THE TRACKS

• To keep a garage door operating smoothly, dissolve grease and dirt inside the garage door tracks annually with a spray solvent; wipe the grime away with a cloth *(right)*.

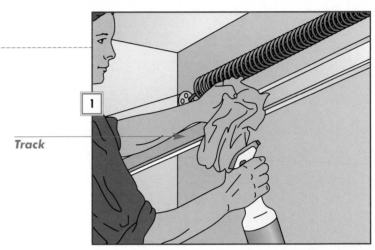

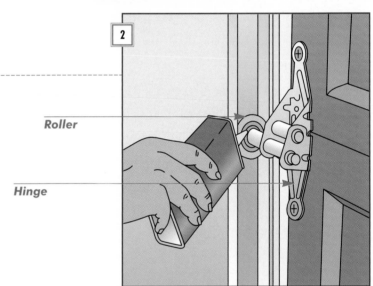

Track

2. LUBRICATING THE DOOR PARTS

• After cleaning the tracks, lubricate all moving parts of a garage door with light machine oil or powdered graphite.

• Apply the lubricant to metal axles and and to the door-roller bearings *(right)*. Also lubricate pivot points on hinges and pulleys. If sticking or squeaks persist, replace the parts *(page 102)*.

Roller

Hinge

3. OILING EXTENSION SPRINGS

Oiling springs prevents rust and squeaks.

• Close the garage door to expand the springs for more thorough lubrication.

• Spray each spring with an even coat of petroleum-based lubricant *(right)*.

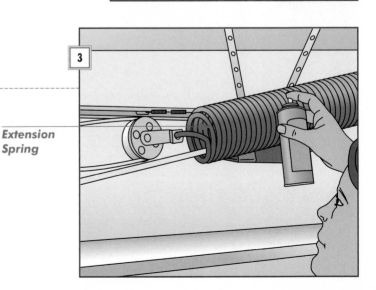

Extension Spring

Adjusting the Opening and Closing Mechanism

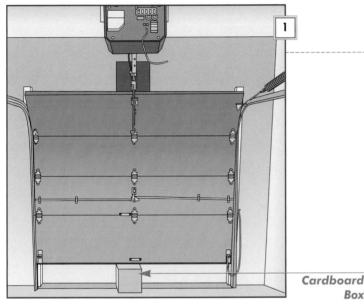

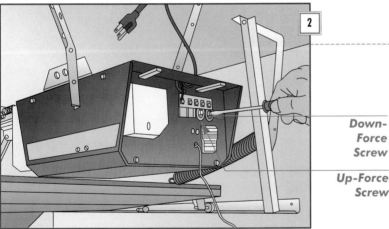

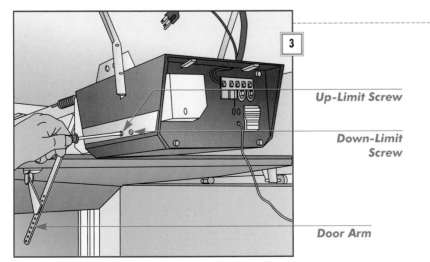

Cardboard Box

Down-Force Screw

Up-Force Screw

Up-Limit Screw

Down-Limit Screw

Door Arm

1. TESTING THE OPENING AND CLOSING MECHANISM

• Open the garage door. If it opens more than 5 feet but fails to open completely, proceed to Step 3.

• Place a cardboard box in the door's path, then close the door via the transmitter or push button. When the bottom of the door touches the box, the door should either stop or reverse direction *(left)*.

• If the door crushes the box or fails to reverse direction, go to Step 2. If it stops short of the box, skip to Step 3.

2. ADJUSTING DOWN-FORCE SENSITIVITY

• Unplug the opener and locate the down-force adjustment screw.

• With a screwdriver, turn the screw counterclockwise 10 degrees *(left)*.

• Plug in the unit and repeat the cardboard box test. Continue adjusting and testing until the door operates properly.

3. ADJUSTING THE LIMIT SCREWS

• If the door fails to open completely, unplug the opener and turn the up-limit screw clockwise *(left)*; one full turn increases travel by 2 inches. Continue adjusting and testing until the door operates properly.

• If the door fails to close completely, unplug the opener and adjust the down-limit screw counterclockwise. Plug in the unit and test it.

• When a door motor continues to hum when the door is fully open or closed, adjust the corresponding limit screw.

4. ADJUSTING THE CHAIN TENSION

A chains that sags more than 1/2 inch below the T-rail may cause a malfunction.

• To tighten a loose chain, loosen the nut on the chain retainer bracket closest to the trolley with a wrench. Then turn the other nut clockwise until the chain hangs 1/2 inch above the base of the T-rail *(right)*.

• Tighten the first nut toward the chain retainer bracket until snug.

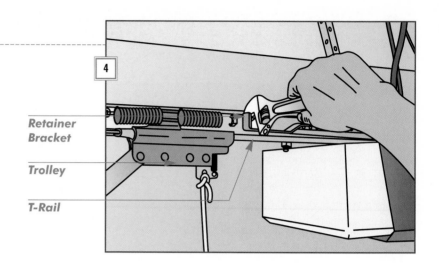

Retainer Bracket

Trolley

T-Rail

Replacing a Worn Roller

1. IMMOBILIZING THE GARAGE DOOR

• Prop the door open with a 2-by-4—unless you're replacing the top roller or unless your door is a swing-up unit. In either of these cases, close the door.

• Unplug the opener.

• As added insurance against accidental closure, firmly screw a C-clamp to the track in front of the top roller *(right)*.

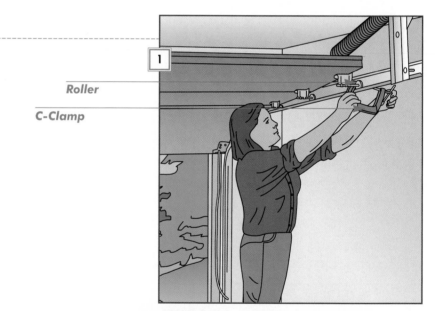

Roller

C-Clamp

2. INSTALLING THE ROLLER

• With a screwdriver or wrench, undo the fasteners holding the hinge-roller to the door.

• Twist the roller out of the track *(right)*, and fit a new roller in place.

• Screw or bolt it to the door.

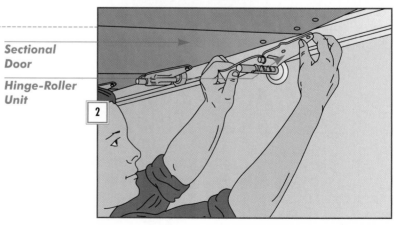

Sectional Door

Hinge-Roller Unit

Installing a New Cable

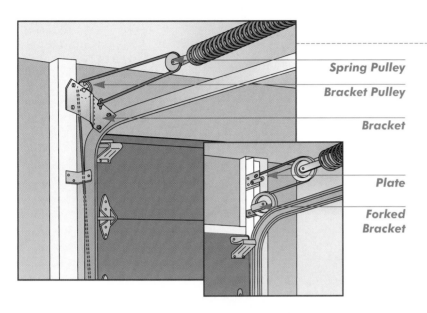

Spring Pulley

Bracket Pulley

Bracket

Plate

Forked Bracket

CABLE CONNECTION

On many garage doors, the cable is knotted to a bracket *(left)*. With other models, the cable may be tied to a plate above the pulley *(inset)*.

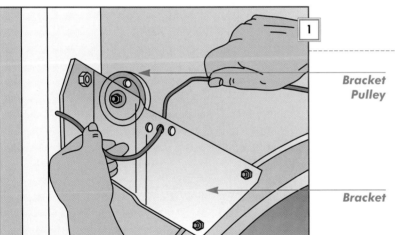

1

Bracket Pulley

Bracket

1. RELEASING THE CABLE AT THE BRACKET END

● Prop and clamp the door open to relax the springs *(page 102)*. Then lift the cable off the bracket pulley with a screwdriver.

● If the pulley wobbles from side to side, replace it *(page 104)*. When cable tension needs adjusting, go to Step 3; but before doing so, replace the cable if it is worn.

● Note the route of the cable; then untie the knot and unthread the cable from the pulleys *(left)*.

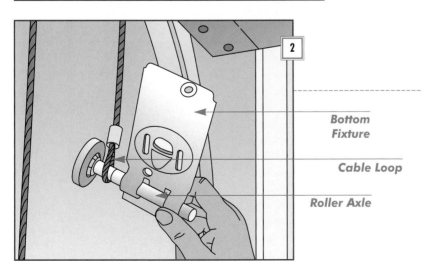

2

Bottom Fixture

Cable Loop

Roller Axle

2. DETACHING THE CABLE AT THE DOOR END

● Unfasten the screws or bolts attaching the bottom roller fixture to the door *(left)*.

● Slide the roller out of the fixture and slip the reinforced cable loop off the roller axle.

● Replace the roller if worn.

3. RE-THREADING THE CABLE AND ADJUSTING TENSION

• Secure the cable to the door at the bottom roller fixture, then thread the cable to the bracket *(right)*.

• Take up any slack in the cable, then tie it to the bracket.

• Test the tension by opening and closing the door; it should move easily on both sides. Adjust the other cable as necessary.

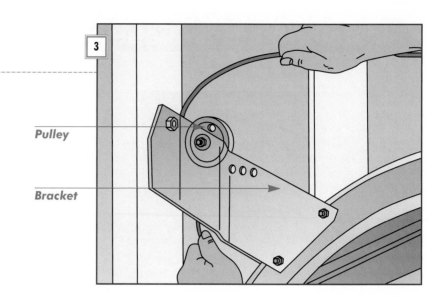

Pulley

Bracket

A New Pulley

BRACKET PULLEY

• With the cable removed from the bracket pulley *(page 103),* unscrew the bolt that holds the pulley on the bracket, using a wrench or nutdriver *(right)*. If the pulley fits into a forked bracket, slip the pulley out of the bracket after you have unbolted it.

• Fit a new pulley in place of the worn one, using the bolt that comes with it.

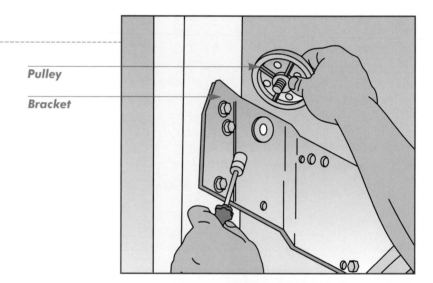

Pulley

Bracket

SPRING PULLEY

• With the cable unthreaded *(page 102),* unhook the forked bracket from the spring and replace it with a new one *(right)*.

• If the replacement does not have a hole on the bracket, slip the spring hook into the space between the pulley and the closed end of the bracket.

• Rethread the cable *(above, Step 3)*.

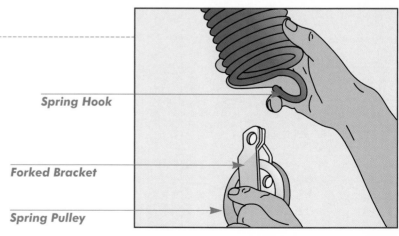

Spring Hook

Forked Bracket

Spring Pulley

Replacing and Adjusting Springs

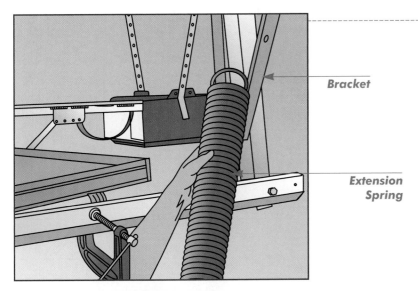

Bracket

Extension Spring

SECTIONAL-DOOR EXTENSION SPRINGS

If the gap between spring coils is more than 1/2 inch—or the springs sag when the door is open—replace both springs.

• Prop the door open *(page 102),* untie the cable *(page 103),* and detach the spring pulley *(page 104).*

• Next, unhook the worn spring from its bracket *(left).*

• Attach the new spring at the back of the track, and hook it to the spring pulley.

• Repeat for the other spring, then adjust the tension *(page 104).*

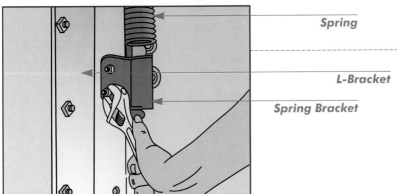

Spring

L-Bracket

Spring Bracket

ADJUSTING TENSION ON SWING-UP DOOR SPRINGS

• Immobilize the door *(page 102, Step 1)* so that the springs are completely relaxed. Locate the end of the spring attached to a movable bracket mounted on an L-bracket (or in holes on the L-bracket).

• To adjust tension, first remove any bolts *(left).* Increase tension by moving the spring bracket up on the L-bracket; decrease tension by moving it down. Adjust both springs.

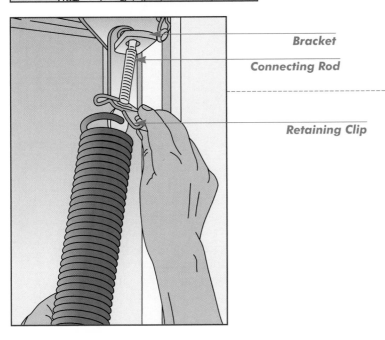

Bracket

Connecting Rod

Retaining Clip

REPLACING SWING-UP DOOR SPRINGS

If the gap between spring coils is more than 1/2 inch in the open position, replace both springs. Detach each spring at its L-bracket end *(above).*

• To remove the spring, hold it in one hand and the retaining clip that connects the spring to the connecting rod in the other; twist the spring until the end slips out of the hole in the connecting rod. Set the retaining clip aside *(left).*

• Install new springs and adjust the tension as explained above.

Cleaning and Lubricating a Drive System

CLEANING THE MECHANISM

One a year, clean the drive screw and track of your garage-door opener.

- First, unplug the machine.

- Then wipe the drive screw and track with a clean rag *(right)*. If the dirt and built-up grime won't come off easily, spray on a cleaning solvent.

- Once clean, spray on a petroleum-based lubricant, plug in the opener, and test it.

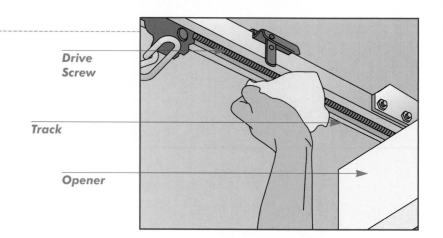

Drive
Screw

Track

Opener

BRUSHING THE DRIVE SCREW

Use a wire brush to remove caked-on dirt and hardened grease that doesn't respond to a rag.

- Unplug the unit.

- Dip the brush in cleaning solvent and vigorously scrub the drive screw *(right)*. Doing so usually defeats even the most stubborn grime.

- Let the drive screw dry; then spray on a petroleum-based lubricant, plug in the opener, and test.

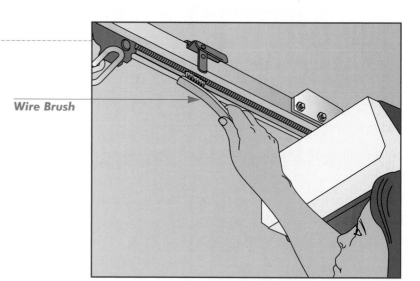

Wire Brush

SPRAY LUBRICANTS

With modern spray lubricants, all it takes is the push of a button to free a binding sash, silence a squeaky hinge, or lubricate the springs on a garage door.

The spray lubricants most useful for maintaining windows and doors are: petroleum-based, silicone-based, and dry-film sprays. Petroleum-based sprays contain a mixture of proprietary petroleum distillates and a propellant, typically carbon dioxide. These sprays are great for lubricating metal parts (like the drive screw or chain on an automatic garage-door opener) and, if applied regularly, will inhibit rust.

Silicone-based sprays excel at lubricating non-metallic surfaces that come into contact with metal, plastic, or wood (such as a window sash and its channel).

Dry-film sprays combine solid lubricants (like graphite), oils, and a propellant. As they dry, they leave behind a thin film of lubrication, making them ideal for linkages such as the scissor arms on a casement window.

Replacing a Garage Door Threshold

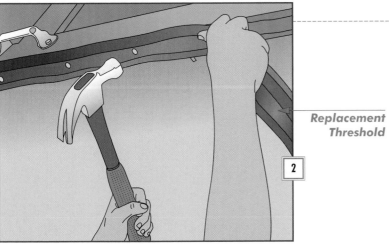

Threshold

Nail

1

1. REMOVING THE OLD THRESHOLD

Unlike most thresholds, which are attached to a floor, the threshold for a garage door is mounted to the bottom of the door so that your car can't travel over it and crush it.

• To replace a threshold that's deteriorated or leaky, start by removing the old one. Many rubber thresholds are simply nailed to the door and can be removed with a pry bar *(left)*.

• If your threshold is attached with screws, remove them with a screwdriver.

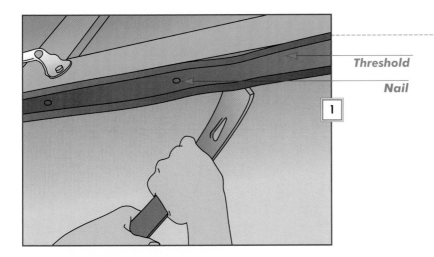

Replacement Threshold

2

2. INSTALLING THE NEW THRESHOLD

• First clean the bottom edge of the door with a wire brush and paint it to prevent moisture from entering the wood.

• Most replacement thresholds are rubber or plastic; you can nail these directly to the bottom of your garage door with galvanized roofing nails *(left)*.

• For a metal door, screw the threshold in place with the screws that come with it.

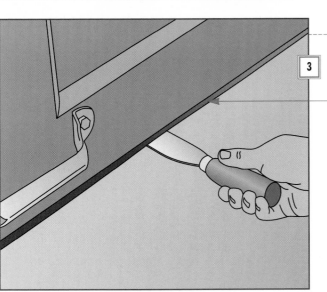

3

Threshold

3. CHECKING FOR GAPS

• Close the garage door and check for gaps every 6 inches by trying to slip a narrow putty knife under the door *(left)*.

• If you encounter a gap, mark it and raise the door.

• Then with a hair dryer, heat the threshold to make it pliable; and, wearing work gloves, bend the lip of the threshold down to eliminate the gap.

• Close the door, check the gap, and adjust as necessary.

FIX IT: Weatherproofing

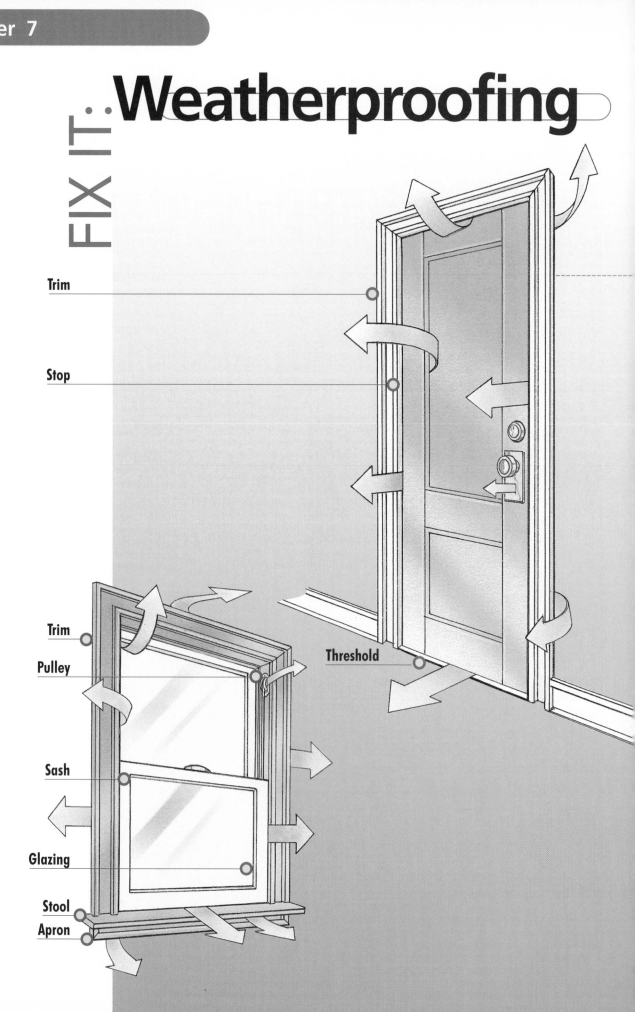

Trim

Stop

Trim

Pulley

Sash

Glazing

Stool

Apron

Threshold

Chapter 7

How They Work

By their very nature, all windows and doors allow air into a room when open; the challenge is preventing unwanted air from slipping past when they're closed.

Air enters around windows through gaps behind the trim, around the stops, between the sash and the jambs, between the upper and lower sash, through pulleys of older double-hung windows, and past old, deteriorating glazing *(left)*.

Around doors, air leaks past stops, through gaps behind trim, under the door, alongside the jambs, and around the glass itself.

Applying weather stripping or caulk or a combination of both usually stops air leaks around doors and windows.

Weather stripping provides a seal for movable joints *(page 116)*, where two surfaces close against each other (a door and a stop) or slide past one another (a window sash and its channel).

Sealants, available as caulk in a tube *(page 112)*, work best on fixed joints: in cracks, along trim edges, or around window sashes that do not open.

Contents

Troubleshooting

Problem	Solution
• **Air leaking around door or window trim**	Caulk gaps around trim and behind jamb **112** •
• **Air leaking around glass pane**	Replace cracked or broken pane or deteriorated glazing compound **88** •
• **Air leaking between window and jamb**	Install cover over exposed pulley or replace or install weather stripping **118** • Replace worn caulk at exposed joints **113** • Reposition window stop to compensate for warped window or house settling **51** •
• **Air leaking between door and jamb**	Install weather stripping **118** • Reposition window stop to compensate for warped window or house settling **51** •
• **Air or water leaking between window sash and stool or sill**	Install weather stripping **118** • Replace sill **15** •
• **Air or water leaking between door and threshold**	Install door sweep **120** • Install door shoe **124** • Install weatherproof threshold **122** •
• **Window or door rattling**	Install weather stripping **118** • Reposition window stop to compensate for warped window or house settling **51** •

Before You Start

Not surprisingly, windows and doors are the most likely source of air leakage into and out of the home.

DETECTING AIR LEAKS

To track down the gaps that let air into your house, tape a strip of kitchen plastic wrap to a coat-hanger. On a windy day, hold the plastic in several positions near each window and door—along trim edges, jamb stops, window-pane edges, and sills. Fluttering of the plastic indicates an area where air is leaking; mark it with chalk. While checking for leaks, also examine any existing weather stripping or sealant. If it is cracked, worn, or deformed, replace it.

STOPPING THE LEAKS

Choose weather stripping to suit the job *(pages 116–117)*. Simple styles, such as V-strips and door sweeps, are the least expensive and tend to develop fewest problems over time. You can replace factory-installed weather stripping, such as the pile strip along the edges of a sliding window sash, when it's worn.

Before You Start Tips:

⋯❖ Seal your home against heat loss well before winter arrives. Many weatherproofing procedures require that you open—or even remove—window sashes or doors.

⋯❖ For best results, weather-strip every surface of a window or door that touches another surface.

TOOLS

Wire brush
Utility knife
Caulking gun
Putty knife
Screwdriver
Long-nose pliers
Hacksaw
Miter box
Handsaw
Electric drill
Circular saw
Carpenter's square
Tin snips
Hammer
Pry bar

MATERIALS

Alcohol
Caulk
Masking tape
Weather stripping
Rubber gloves
Galvanized nails

SAFETY FIRST

When using sealants or caulk, follow the manufacturer's application instructions, wear gloves, and always provide adequate ventilation.

Common Sealants

100% Silicone

Great for interior and exterior trim, sills, thresholds, and glass panes; can be applied in cold weather. Remains extremely flexible, yet shrinks the least of the caulks shown here. Fills gaps up to 1/2 inch wide. Colorless and durable (paintable type may be less durable). When applying, wear eye protection and use only in a well-ventilated area.

Acrylic Latex Caulk

Good for sealing windows, doors, trim, and corner joints; can be applied only above 40°F. Less flexible than silicone, but costs less. Good adhesion, but will shrink; best for gaps less than 3/8 inch wide. Comes in colors, is moderately durable, and may be painted.

Acrylic Latex Caulk Plus Silicone

Works well for sealing windows and doors and for filling gaps up to 3/8 inch wide; can be applied only above 40°F. Contains a small amount of silicone (typically less than 2%), which improves adhesion but not flexibility. Available in a variety of colors, but also may be painted.

Vinyl Adhesive Caulk

Good when you need a combination of high adhesion and sealing such as replacing a double-pane window in a frame. The caulk both seals and bonds the parts together, making for a stronger window or door. Moderate flexibility, comes in some colors, and may be painted. Cures in 12 to 48 hours, but may be painted after 1 hour.

Elastomeric Indoor/Outdoor Sealant

Dries tack-free in less than 10 minutes, but can fill only gaps less than 1/4 inch wide. Not as flexible as the other caulks but is quite durable when dry. Clear but paintable. Contains irritating chemicals; wear gloves and eye protection and work only in a well-ventilated area.

CHOOSING AMONG SEALANTS

The chart above describes the five most common sealants used for windows and doors. You can use any of them indoors or out; and with some exceptions, they are mostly interchangeable. The biggest differences among them are in gap-filling capability and durability.

Silicone caulk fills the widest gaps and is the most durable, often guaranteed by the manufacturers to stand up to the elements for 10 to 25 years—up to twice as long as other kinds of caulk. The drawback to silicone caulk is that it costs two to five times as much as the next best caulk, acrylic latex caulk.

Adhesion is a measure of how well the sealant sticks to a surface to make a tight seal, not its ability to act as a glue (although vinyl adhesive caulk does offer a bond similar to glue). High flexibility and low shrinkage are more important for exterior work, where joints expand and contract with changes in temperature and humidity.

Caulking Minor Gaps in a Wall

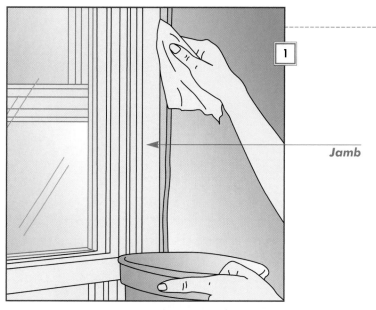

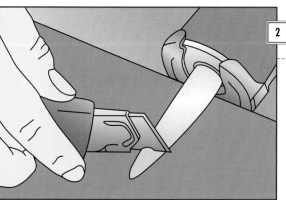

1. PREPARING THE SURFACE

To stop air leaks around a window, look for gaps behind the trim.

- Score the paint between the trim and the wall; pry off the trim with a utility bar, protecting the wall with a wood shim.

- With a wire brush or utility knife, scrape old caulk and paint off of exposed surfaces.

- Clean the area with a mild soap-and-water solution *(left)*.

- When dry, wipe the surface with a cloth dampened with alcohol to remove all traces of moisture and adhesive.

2. PREPARING THE CAULK

- Cut off the tip of a tube of silicone or water-based acrylic caulk with a utility knife *(left)* so its opening is slightly smaller than the width of the crack.

- Break the foil seal at the base of the tip by inserting a long nail or a piece of stiff wire.

3. SEALING A SMALL CRACK

- For deep gaps or hollows, first stuff closed-cell foam rope into the opening with a screwdriver.

- Then lay a continuous bead of caulk along the crack with a caulking gun *(left)*. Move the gun steadily, completing one side at a time. To stop the flow of caulk, turn the gun's plunger handle down or snap the release lever.

- Re-install the trim, driving slightly larger finishing nails through the old holes.

Jamb

Foam Rope

Foam to Fill Large Gaps

1. APPLYING THE FOAM

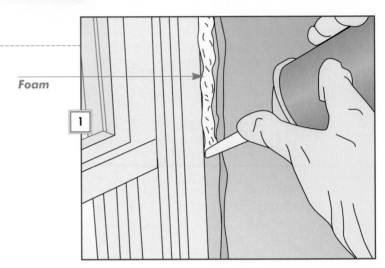

Foam

- After prying off the trim, open the window for ventilation, and put on rubber gloves and safety goggles.

- Attach the applicator tube to the nozzle of the can, shake it, and turn it at a 45-degree angle.

- Insert the tip into the gap *(right)* and press the nozzle. Fill no more than half the depth of the gap; the foam will expand to fill it. Release the trigger 5 inches before the end of the gap, but continue to move the applicator to the end.

2. TRIMMING THE WASTE

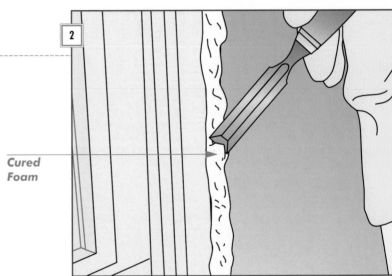

- Allow the foam to cure for 8 hours, or overnight if possible. It will change in consistency from whipped cream to solid sponge.

Cured Foam

- Trim off excess foam with a sharp chisel or utility knife *(right)*.

- Re-install the trim, driving slightly larger finishing nails through the old holes.

Ron's TRADE SECRETS

PRESERVING CAULK WITH A WIRE CAP

Virtually anything that is dispensed with a caulking gun will harden if the cartridge tip is left exposed. I can't tell you how many half-used tubes of caulk I've saved over the years just by screwing a wire cap onto the tip *(right)*. Wire caps are available in the electrical aisle at your local hardware store or home center. They are color-coded according to size; gray ones fit nicely over the trimmed cartridge tip.

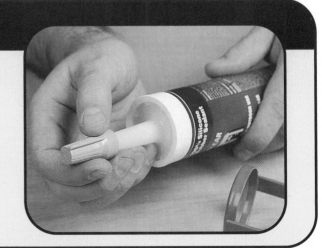

Plugging Air Leaks around Trim

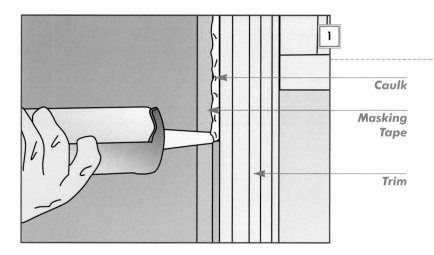

Caulk

Masking
Tape

Trim

1. APPLYING CAULK AROUND TRIM

Although caulking *behind* the trim is the best way to stop air leakage, caulking *around* it saves removing the trim.

● Clean the outer edge of the trim with mild soap solution, rinse, and dry. Then wipe the joint with a cloth dampened with alcohol.

● Affix masking tape to the wall and trim to maintain straight edges.

● With a caulking gun, lay a continuous bead between the trim and the wall *(left).*

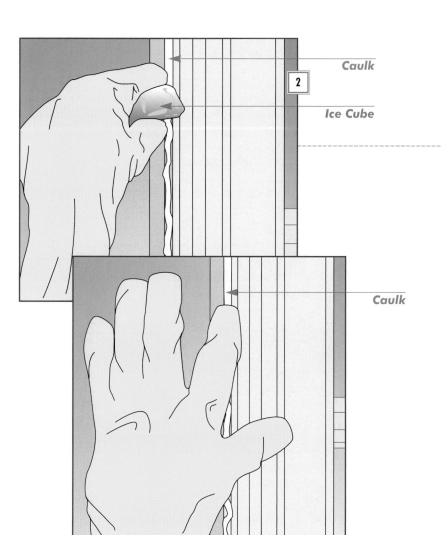

Caulk

Ice Cube

Caulk

2. SMOOTHING THE CAULK

● Let the caulk dry until it is no longer tacky but has not yet formed a skin.

● Then, wearing rubber gloves, gently slide an ice cube over the center of the bead of caulk *(left, top)* to make a smooth, slightly concave surface.

● Alternatively, smooth the caulk using a gloved finger moistened with a soap-and-water solution *(left, bottom).*

● If you applied masking tape, pull it off. Cut away excess caulk with a sharp utility knife.

Weather Stripping

Carefully match weather stripping to its job. Listed below are a wide variety of weather-stripping products, along with their recommended applications, installation procedures, and relative durability.

For best results, weather-strip all contacting surfaces of windows and doors. Use a sliding seal, such as V-strip, in areas where two parts slide past each other—in a sash channel, for example. Use a compressible seal, such as a foam strip, where two parts press against each other—like a door stop.

Give special attention to the bottom of an exterior door. Space between the door and threshold lets in not only air but also water and dirt.

TYPE	APPLICATION	INSTALLATION	DURABILITY
Open-cell foam strip	A compressible seal for interior doors, along closing side of stop.	Self-adhesive; may be nailed or stapled for better adhesion (*page 118*).	Wears out quickly and deforms easily. Must be checked and replaced regularly.
Closed-cell foam strip	A compressible seal for moderately even gaps along stops of hinged windows and doors, and on bottom rail of double-hung windows.	Self-adhesive; may be nailed or stapled in place for better adhesion (*page 114*).	Long-lasting, retains shape and flexibility. Loosens and wears quickly on sliding surfaces.
Tubular gasket	A compressible seal for irregular gaps along door and window stops, and on bottom rail of double-hung windows.	Self-adhesive, or nailed, or stapled in place. Less noticeable if installed on exterior side.	Long-lasting, retains shape. Plastic gaskets are less flexible and less resistant to cold than rubber ones.
Grooved gasket	A compressible seal for metal casement, jalousie, and some multi-vent awning windows.	Snaps over metal or glass slat edges and may be secured with special adhesive. Usually made-to-measure.	Long-lasting, retains shape.
V-strip	A sliding seal for sliding surfaces of most doors and windows. Plastic V-strip may also be applied to compression surfaces.	Metal V-strip is nailed in place. Plastic V-strip is self-adhesive (*page 119*).	Long-lasting. Metal V-strip may deform, loosening from nails.
Pile strip	A sliding seal used as a replacement for factory-installed weather stripping on metal windows.	Self-adhesive or snap-in. Must use correct size (*page 121*).	Moderately long-lasting. Plastic film insert on some types improves seal.

Weather Stripping

The simple addition of a door sweep *(page 120)* will close off a narrow gap. You can obtain an even better seal by installing a door shoe *(page 124)* or by replacing a worn threshold with a weatherproof threshold *(page 122)*.

After choosing weather stripping, take time to prepare the surface and install it correctly. Carefully remove all traces of old caulk or weather stripping with a utility knife or single-edged razor blade. Remove old adhe-

sive with rubbing alcohol or mineral spirits. Wash the surfaces with a soap solution; residue from mineral spirits will damage many synthetic products.

TYPE	APPLICATION	INSTALLATION	DURABILITY
Spring-loaded jamb strip	A compressible seal for hinged doors and windows.	Screwed to jamb through attachment strip *(page 120)*. Caulking behind attachment strip improves the seal.	Long-lasting.
Magnetic jamb strip	A compressible seal for hinged steel doors and windows or, if a steel strip is attached, for wood windows and doors.	Screwed to jamb through attachment strip. Factory-installed on prehung units.	Long-lasting. Seal may deteriorate in extremely cold weather.
Partial threshold	A compressible seal for doors with no threshold, such as storm doors.	Screwed to door sill through metal plate.	Long-lasting. Has a replaceable rubber or plastic insert.
Complete threshold	A compressible and sliding seal for replacement of a worn wood threshold.	Screwed to door sill through metal plate *(page 122)*. Door may need to be trimmed.	Long-lasting. Has a replaceable rubber or plastic insert.
Door sweep	A compressible and sliding seal for narrow gaps at bottom of exterior doors. May drag on carpeted floors.	Screwed to door bottom inside, through metal or plastic attachment strip *(page 120)*. May be adjusted if gap widens .	Moderately long-lasting. Has a replaceable rubber, plastic, or pile insert.
Door shoe	A sliding seal for narrow or wide gaps at bottom of exterior doors. Comes in several styles.	Screwed to door bottom inside and outside, through metal or plastic attachment strip *(page 124)*. Door may need to be trimmed.	Long-lasting. Has a replaceable rubber, plastic, or pile insert.

Weather-Stripping Wood Windows and Doors

PULLEY COVERS

Seal air leaks around a pulley with a self-adhesive pulley cover.

● Clean around the pulley with alcohol, then apply the self-adhesive gasket to the back of the pulley cover, leaving the backing paper undisturbed.

● Position the cover over the pulley and snap the sash cord into the opening in the bottom of the cover *(right)*.

● Outline the cover with a pencil. Then peel off the backing and press the cover against the sash channel.

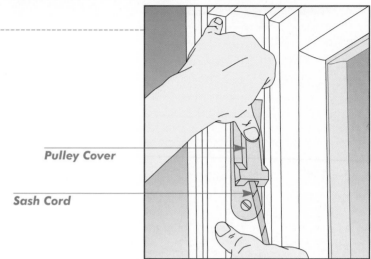

Pulley Cover

Sash Cord

ADDING A FOAM STRIP TO THE BOTTOM OF A SASH

● Remove loose paint and old weather stripping or caulk with a paint scraper.

● Wash the surface with a soap-and-water solution. Rinse and dry it, then wipe it with a cloth dampened with alcohol.

● To install the foam strip, start at one end and slowly peel off the paper backing as you press the strip in place *(right)*.

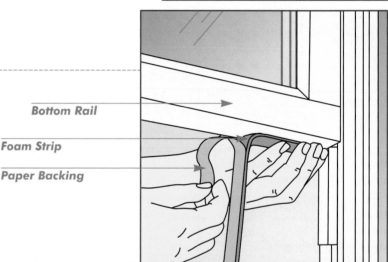

Bottom Rail

Foam Strip

Paper Backing

 Ron's TRADE SECRETS

SNAKING SELF-ADHESIVE STRIPS

Here's how I prevent pressure-sensitive adhesive on weather stripping from sticking as I slide it between the sash and jamb of a double-hung window. First, I cut the backing paper about a foot from the top. Beginning at the cut, I peel the paper upward and fold it over the top *(right)*. Then I raise the lower sash and slip the weather stripping up between the sash and the jamb. After removing the backing paper from the lower section of the strip and pressing it to the jamb, I lower the sash, pull off the rest of the backing paper, and press the upper section in place.

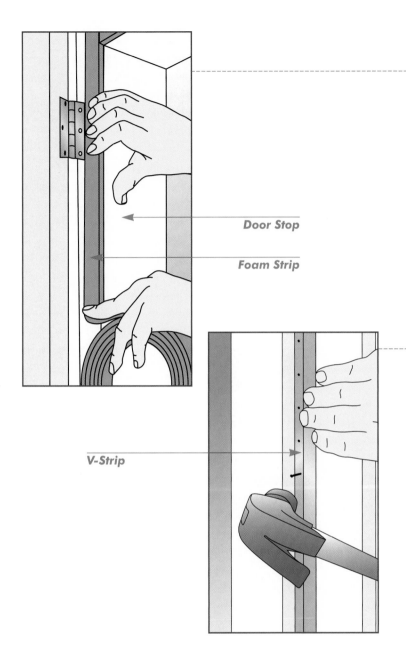

Door Stop

Foam Strip

V-Strip

APPLYING FOAM STRIPS TO A DOOR STOP

Self-adhesive foam strips are ideal for the stops of doors *(left)* and windows, where screws would prevent the door from closing all the way.

● Apply the strips as described on page 118 for a bottom sash.

● Cut the strip with a utility knife after applying it to each straight surface.

● Secure the strip with staples for a longer-lasting grip.

V-STRIPS IN SASH CHANNELS

Metal and plastic V-strips are interchangeable. The metal variety is shown here and in the illustration below. Staple plastic V-strips for better adhesion.

● Prepare the surface as for foam weather stripping *(page 118)*.

● Measure a sash stile and add 2 inches. With tin snips, cut two V-strips to length.

● Raise the lower sash, position the strips in the lower sash channel, and snake the strips up between the raised sash and the jamb.

● Nail the strips in place *(left)*, spacing the the nails at 1-inch intervals.

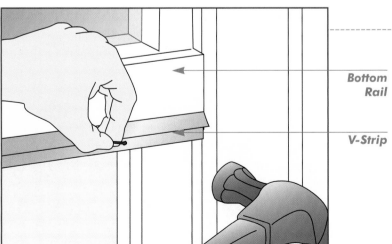

Bottom Rail

V-Strip

V-STRIPS ON BOTTOM RAIL

● Measure the bottom rail of the upper sash and cut a V-strip to this length.

● Position the strip along the bottom rail, with the V opening downward *(left)*, and nail it in place.

V-STRIP ON A DOOR STOP

Metal and plastic V-strips are interchangeable. The plastic variety is shown here. Staple plastic V-strips for better adhesion.

● For a door, fasten V-strips to the jamb with the V pointed away from the stop *(right)*, leaving a gap at the strike plate. There, attach a short piece of V-strip to the stop. You can also apply V-strips to other compressions joints, such as the bottom rail of a lower window sash.

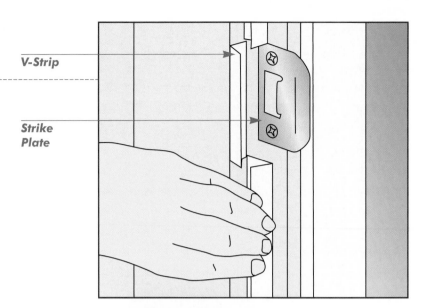

V-Strip

Strike Plate

INSTALLING SPRING-LOADED WEATHER STRIPPING

● With a hacksaw, cut a strip to match the height of the jamb.

● Push thumbtacks through screw holes to hold the strip on the jamb, with the contact surface against the door and the spring depressed one-third of its travel.

● Remove one tack at a time and fasten the strip with screws *(right)*.

● Cut and position a strip for the head jamb using the same procedure.

● Use a foam strip or a V-strip for the hinge side of the door.

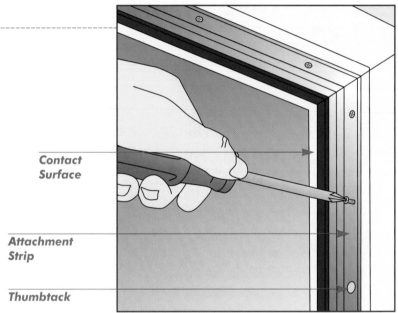

Contact Surface

Attachment Strip

Thumbtack

ADDING A DOOR SWEEP

To block a gap between the door and the threshold, install a door sweep with a replaceable insert. Buy one to fit the door or cut it to size with a hacksaw.

● Close the door and place the door sweep against the interior bottom edge of the door, ensuring that the flexible insert covers the gap entirely.

● Mark the positions of the screw holes in the attachment strip, drill pilot holes, then fasten the sweep with screws *(right)*.

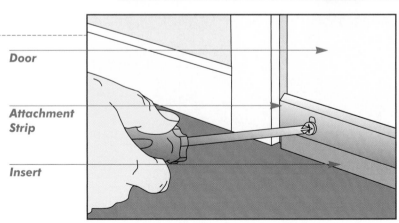

Door

Attachment Strip

Insert

Resealing Metal Windows and Doors

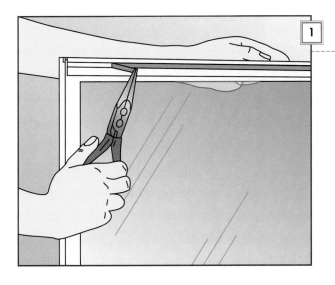

1. REMOVING A FACTORY-INSTALLED PILE STRIP

Most metal windows come with factory-installed pile strips.

● To replace a matted or worn strip, start by removing the sash from its tracks *(page 25)*.

● Check both ends of the pile strip for two tiny metal tabs that may be securing it. Bend them up gently with a screwdriver.

● With long-nose pliers, grasp the strip and pull it out of its channel *(left)*.

● Take the strip to a window repair specialist for an exact replacement.

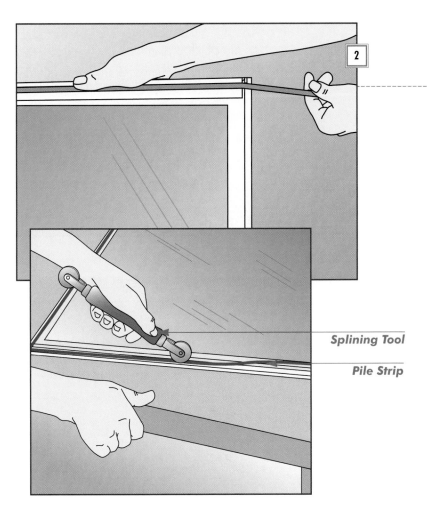

Splining Tool

Pile Strip

2. REPLACING THE PILE STRIP

● Clean the pile strip channel with an old toothbrush.

● Cut the new strip with scissors to the length of the channel.

● Feed a thick pile strip back into its channel from one end *(left, top)*. To install a thin pile strip, place it over the channel, and snap the strip into the channel with the concave end of a splining tool *(left, bottom)*.

● Bend the metal tabs back over the ends of the strip, and replace the sash in its track in the frame.

Installing a Weatherproof Threshold

1. CUTTING THROUGH THE OLD THRESHOLD

- Cut away old caulk from around the threshold with a utility knife.

- If stops are nailed or screwed to the jambs, carefully remove them *(page 51)*.

- If you can tap the threshold out with a mallet, do so, then skip to Step 3.

- If the jambs have built-in stops, cut part-way through the threshold *(right)*, taking care not to cut into the sill beneath it.

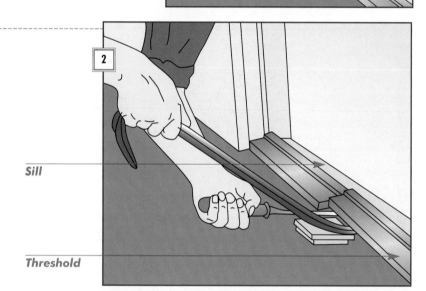

Threshold

2. REMOVING THE OLD THRESHOLD

- Push the end of a screwdriver under the cut edge of the threshold to raise it for a pry bar. Insert the pry bar, placing scraps of wood under it to protect the sill *(right)*.

- Pry up the threshold.

- Once raised, the two sections should break apart; if they don't, cut through them with a saw and pull the threshold pieces out by hand.

- Then cut or pull any protruding nails *(page 16)*.

Sill

Threshold

Ron's TRADE SECRETS

PREVENTING FLOOR DAMAGE

Even the most skilled carpenter runs the risk of damaging a floor when cutting through a door threshold. To keep this from happening to me, I tape scraps of plastic laminate to both sides of the threshold *(right)*. Then I begin cutting the middle of the threshold. When the saw teeth start to score the laminate, it's time to stop.

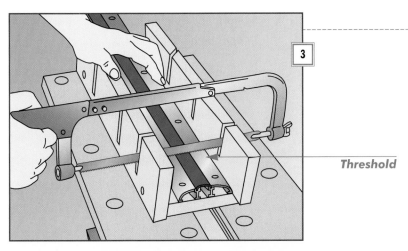

Threshold

3. CUTTING THE NEW THRESHOLD

• Measure the old threshold, inserting the saw you used to cut it between the two pieces to compensate for the wood you removed. Mark the new threshold at this length.

• Place the threshold in a miter box and cut it with a hacksaw *(left)*.

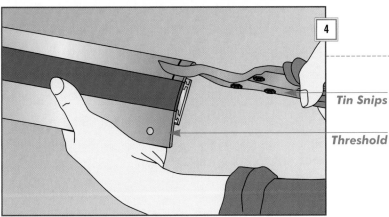

Tin Snips

Threshold

4. FITTING THE THRESHOLD WITH TIN SNIPS

• Use a square to mark any notches that the threshold needs to fit door jamb's contours.

• If the threshold metal is thin, cut the notches with tin snips *(left)*. Otherwise, cut them with a hacksaw, utilizing the miter box whenever possible.

• Position the threshold on the floor and close the door to ensure even contact with the rubber or plastic insert.

• If the door binds on the threshold, trim or cut the door to fit *(pages 50 and 54)*.

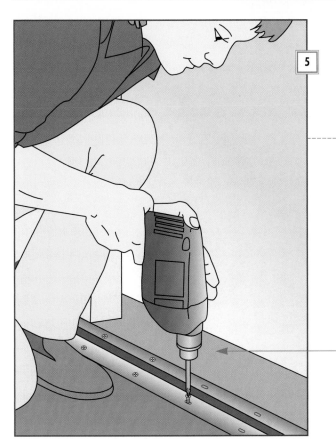

Sill

5. INSTALLING THE NEW THRESHOLD

• Mark positions of screw holes. Then drill pilot holes for the threshold screws, wrapping masking tape around the bit as a depth gauge.

• Apply silicone caulk under the edges of the threshold and screw it to the sill *(left)*.

• If you removed the door stops in Step 1, re-install them *(page 51)*.

Adding a Door Shoe

1. MEASURING THE SHOE DEPTH

If there is a gap between the door and the threshold, install a door shoe to stop air and water leakage.

● For the style shown here, hold the door shoe in place on the door and measure from the door bottom to the shoe bottom *(right)*.

● Remove the shoe, close the door, and mark this measurement on the door near each corner, measuring from the top of the threshold.

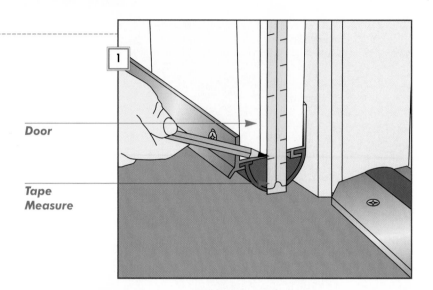

Door

Tape Measure

2. CUTTING THE DOOR

● Remove the door from its hinges *(page 46)* and set it on sawhorses.

● With a straightedge, draw a line connecting the two marks on the door.

● Clamp a straight piece of wood to the door, parallel to the line, as a guide for a circular saw, and cut along the line *(right)*.

● Smooth the rough edge with sandpaper, and seal the door bottom with water-repellent finish or varnish.

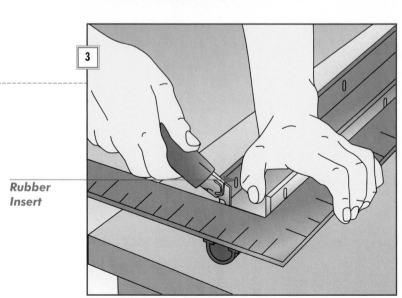

Guide

3. TRIMMING THE DOOR SHOE

● Measure the width of the door and mark this measurement on the door shoe.

● Slip the rubber insert partway out of the shoe. Cut through the rubber with a utility knife, using a square as a guide *(right)*.

● Return the rubber insert to its original position, then cut through the attachment strips with a hacksaw.

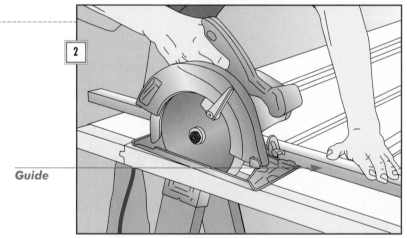

Rubber Insert

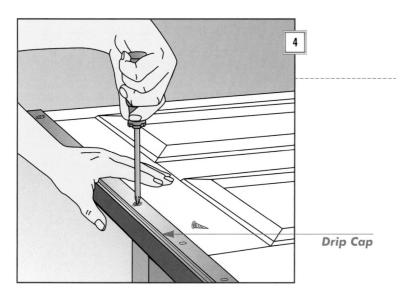

Drip Cap

4. INSTALLING THE DOOR SHOE

- Position the shoe on the bottom of the door, with the drip cap on the exterior side of the door.

- Make starter holes for the screws with an awl in the center of the elongated attachment holes, and screw the attachment strips to the door *(left)*.

- Rehang the door.

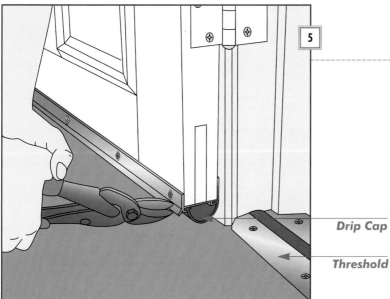

Drip Cap

Threshold

5. TRIMMING THE DRIP CAP

- If the drip cap prevents the door from closing fully, simply trim the drip cap at both ends with tin snips *(left)*.

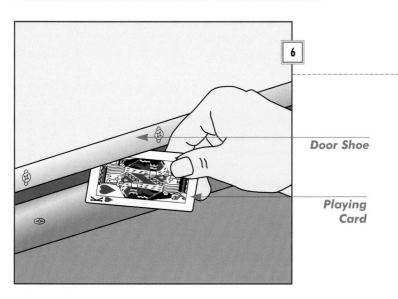

Door Shoe

Playing Card

6. CHECKING FOR GAPS

- Try to slide a playing card in between the door shoe and the threshold *(left)*. If the card slips through anywhere, loosen the screws and adjust the attachment strip to close the gap.

Index

TIME®
LIFE

Time-Life Books
is a division of Time Life Inc.

Time Life Inc.

George Artandi
President and CEO

Time-Life Books

Stephen R. Frary
President

Neil Kagan
Publisher/Managing Editor

Steven A. Schwartz
Vice President, Marketing

How To Fix It:

Windows & Doors

Lee Hassig
Editor

Wells P. Spence
Marketing Manager

Kate McConnell
Design Director

Janet Johnson
Special Contributor (design)

Christopher Hearing
Director of Finance

Marjann Caldwell
Patricia Pascale
Directors of Book Production

Betsi McGrath
Director of Publishing Technology

John Conrad Weiser
Director of Photography
and Research

Barbara Levitt
Director of Editorial Administration

Marlene Zack
Production Manager

James King
Quality Assurance Manager

Louise D. Forstall
Chief Librarian

Butterick Media

Staff for Major Appliances

Rick Peters
Editor

Caroline Politi
Director of Book Production

Ben Ostasiewski
Art Director

David Joinnides
Page Layout

Jim Kingsepp
Technical Consultant

Barbara M. Webb
Copy Editor

Nan Badgett
Indexer

Tom Perez
Set Construction

Lillian Esposito
Production Editor

Art Joinnides
President

Picture Credits

Fil Hunter
Cover Photograph

Bob Crimi
Geoff McCormack
Linda Richards
Joseph Taylor
Illustration

Brian Kraus
Juan Rios
"Butterick Media"
Interior Photographs

Illustration Credit

**Caradco Wood Windows
and Patio Doors**
Page 82

Library of Congress
Cataloging-in-Publication Data
Windows & doors / by the editors of
Time-Life Books :
with trade secrets from Ron Hazelton.
    p. cm. -- (How to Fix It)
    Includes index.
    ISBN 0-7835-5652-7
    1. Windows---Maintenance and repair.
2. Doors-- Maintenance & Repair. I. Hazelton, Ron.
II. Time-Life Books. III. Series.
TH2270.W63 1998   98-27068
690'.0823--dc21   CIP